Arthur Eve

Moises Morales

Polly Baca-Barragan

bajo Con
os Politicos

Six politicians who believe they can and will "make a difference" are profiled in this stirring collection, marked by moments of unusual candor and wit. These are risk-takers who speak frankly about a life in politics and have chosen to put themselves on the line.

☆ Scare-tactics from the opposing side have not stifled third-party candidate MOISES MORALES.

☆ Southern NANCY STEVENSON describes what it's like to be a woman running against three men.

☆ A charismatic black spokesman, ARTHUR EVE knows how to run an effective street campaign against the tough "machine."

☆ New politician-superstar BILL BRADLEY makes connections between politics and basketball.

☆ Former 1960's student radical, TOM HAYDEN now talks about running for senate and keeping his radicalism alive.

☆ Chicano and activist, POLLY BACA-BARRAGAN walks a thin line serving her conservative district.

Elizabeth Levy and Mara Miller have compiled a timely and thought-provoking book for young people and adults. Whether or not you agree with these six politicians, they are sure to win your confidence and respect.

by Elizabeth Levy

LAWYERS FOR THE PEOPLE

by Elizabeth Levy & Mara Miller

DOCTORS FOR THE PEOPLE

POLITICIANS FOR THE PEOPLE

Politicians for the People

SIX WHO STAND FOR CHANGE

Elizabeth Levy & Mara Miller

Alfred A. Knopf · New York

Acknowledgments

Our thanks to George Vickers, Jeff Miller, and Kenneth Mac Kenzie; to Betsy Wright and Cindy Ullman of the National Women's Education Fund; to Blair MacInnes and Kathleen Lynch; and to Dr. Hunter S. Thompson, to whom this book is dedicated.

ACKNOWLEDGMENTS: Thanks are due to the following for permission to reprint previously published material:

Dissent Magazine: Excerpt from "Dissent" by Tom Hayden.

Farrar, Straus & Giroux, Inc.: Excerpt from *A Sense of Where You Are* by John McPhee. Copyright © 1965, 1978 by John McPhee.

The New American Library, Inc.: Excerpt from *A Prophetic Minority* by Jack Newfield. Copyright © 1966 by Jack Newfield. Reprinted by arrangement with The New American Library, Inc., New York, N.Y.

Quadrangle/The New York Times Book Co., Inc.: Excerpt from *Life on the Run* by Bill Bradley (Quadrangle, 1976), pp. 35–36. Copyright © 1976 by Bill Bradley. Reprinted by permission of Times Books, a division of Quadrangle/The New York Times Book Co., Inc. from *Life On the Run* by Bill Bradley.

Quadrangle/The New York Times Book Co., Inc.: Excerpt from *A Time to Die* by Tom Wicker (Quadrangle, 1975), p. 240. Copyright © 1975 by Tom Wicker. Reprinted by permission of Times Books, a division of Quadrangle/The New York Times Book Co., Inc. from *A Time to Die* by Tom Wicker.

George Vickers: Excerpt from an unpublished interview with Tom Hayden, Venice, California, August 23, 1971.

This is a Borzoi Book published by Alfred A. Knopf, Inc.

Library of Congress Cataloging in Publication Data

Levy, Elizabeth. Politicians for the people. Summary: Presents career biographies of men and women noted for their non-traditional approach to politics. 1. Politicians—United States—Biography—Juvenile literature.   2. United States —Politics and government—1945-   —Juvenile literature. [1. Politicians] I. Miller, Mara. II. Title, E840.6.L48 1979 329'.0092'2 [920] 79–2198
ISBN 0–394–84068–2   ISBN 0–394–94068–7 lib. bdg.

Jacket and book design by Mina Greenstein. 1 2 3 4 5 6 5 7 9 10

Contents

☆

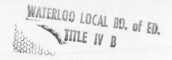

Introduction
3

MOISES MORALES
"In the End, There's Just the People"
•9•

NANCY STEVENSON
*"They Want Their Women Ladylike
in This State"*
•26•

ARTHUR EVE
*"Give the Brothers and Sisters
Some Role in the Struggle"*
•44•

BILL BRADLEY
"The Great White Hope"
•63•

TOM HAYDEN
*"You Can't Personally Start a Movement,
No Matter How Much You Want It"*
•82•

POLLY BACA-BARRAGAN
*"I Never Thought I'd Ever Meet a Politician,
Let Alone Be One"*
•99•

Politicians for the People

Introduction

─────────── ☆ ───────────

We grew up politically in the Sixties. It was a time
when the political system seemed to be opening up to
include men and women who stood for dramatic,
radical change. It was not just that real change *seemed*
to be taking place; it *did* happen. The movement to
end the war in Vietnam, the civil rights movement,
the women's movement, the student and poor people's
movements—all these made concrete gains. It seemed
to us then that politics would be different in the future.
We believed that our generation's sheer size and
political involvement had created a groundswell for
change so powerful that leaders could emerge in the
1970's who would embody these changes and together
we would go even further.

It hasn't happened. In order to find six politicians we
wanted to include in this book we had to look hard. On
the national scene, no leader stood out. We had to go
to state and local governments to find potential leaders,
men and women who were not afraid to say, "People

are suffering, poverty exists, prejudice and self-interest play too large a role in how we govern, things can be made better."

Many of the people in this book will be as new to you as they were to us. Others will be more familiar. We knew we wanted to include Tom Hayden. His work in the early days of the civil rights movement in the South, his organizing of the student movement and later the antiwar movement, and his recent involvement in party politics (running for the U.S. Senate in California) made him an obvious choice. Hayden's access to national Democratic politics came, as he admits, with his marriage to movie star Jane Fonda; but his sharp instinct for justice predates this and remains uncurbed. As a college student, Hayden went to Georgia and Mississippi to report and take part in the struggle for human rights going on there. He has been beaten, jailed, and convicted for his political beliefs and the extent of his social criticism. We sensed as we talked to him that Hayden will continue to identify with outsiders, with the have-nots in America.

Bill Bradley, the new U.S. senator from New Jersey, is the only other politician profiled in this book whom most readers will recognize. A superstar basketball player in college and later with the New York Knicks, Bradley achieved a national reputation in sports, yet he was always up-front about his desire to run for political office. Bradley feels that his years in pro basketball, a sport dominated by black players, helped make him aware of the deep divisions in our society. He wants to do something about them.

Nancy Stevenson is the new lieutenant-governor of South Carolina. An intelligent woman with southern political savvy, she bucked the odds against a liberal woman running for statewide office in a conservative southern state—and won. A staunch advocate of human rights, she is a creative thinker who looks at old problems in new ways. She is able to cut through the weeds that ensnare most politicians. She is a novelist, and there's something engaging and refreshing about her approach to government.

Polly Baca-Barragan, a state senator in Colorado, is absorbed by politics. An activist Chicano woman, she has not lost one campaign in her elective career and now holds a leadership post in her state's legislature, a job usually reserved for men. She's done all this without compromising her convictions on human issues.

Moises Morales is a radical who stands outside two-party politics. He ran for sheriff in New Mexico on the slate of La Raza Unida, a loosely knit group of people who live and work cooperatively, running a health clinic and farming coop and fighting for land reform in the Southwest. Morales's involvement has been with an often violent kind of politics. When he was only nineteen, he was bodyguard to Reies Tijerina, a radical Chicano preacher. Morales took part in the Courthouse Raid of Tierra Amarilla, an event that made national news headlines in 1967.

Arthur Eve was an unexpected winner of the Democratic primary for mayor of Buffalo. He has been a member of the New York State Assembly for over ten years, and he's been a prime mover in getting black and Puerto Rican politicians to work together as a cohesive political force for change. Eve, who has fought machine politics all his life, combines a strong sense of outrage at the conditions around him with a love of the nitty-gritty of electioneering. What's also exciting about Eve is that he's not interested merely in getting out the vote for himself. He loves to teach others—particularly black candidates and would-be candidates—how to do what he has done.

Each of these people came out of a movement for change. But we would be kidding you as well as ourselves if we didn't point out one fundamental difference: three are outsiders in our political system, and three are not.

Bill Bradley, Nancy Stevenson, and Polly Baca-Barragan are winners. They have been victorious in their political campaigns and represent, for us, the best the two-party system has to offer. As we got to know them, we sensed that each was aware of what was wrong and should be changed; and each was excited about the possibility of what might be done. But their criticisms and proposals kept within the so-called feasible limits of what they felt the voters would tolerate.

Moises Morales, Tom Hayden, and Arthur Eve are rank outsiders. Their criticism of American life is far-reaching and unwelcome. Their outrage and the way in which they express it, as well as the solutions they offer, seem threatening to many voters and certainly to many politicians. They have all lost their major campaigns.

We wish all six people in this book were in office today. You always hear that "if you don't like what those in office are doing, work to elect someone whose views you do like." In the Sixties we saw that change did not happen that way. Only when masses of people got together to demonstrate against prejudice, war, and poverty did anything happen. Change came from the people, not from the "leaders."

Believing then that the impetus for change comes from below, why did we limit our profiles to those who have run for office? That's a hard question to answer. First, when there is no active mass movement toward change, traditional politics becomes practically the only visible game in town. The late 1970's is such a time. Second, we admit to being what might be called "political junkies." We may not always find candidates we want to vote for, much less work for, but we are never more happy than when we are working for a candidate who will "make a difference."

You will find several biases in this book. On some issues, we just don't see two sides. For example, we support the Equal Rights Amendment, are against the death penalty, are for the right to abortion, and have a commitment to poor people and the improvement of human services. We would only vote for men and women committed to these issues. You will only find in this book people who share that commitment.

To varying degrees, our six politicians are risk-takers. They have chosen to put themselves on the line, asking people to vote for them *and* what they stand for. It isn't done that often these days.

We wanted to find some politicians you could have confidence in, could respect, and could be excited by—whether you agreed with them or not. We think we have done just that.

Moises Morales

"In the End, There's Just the People"

Violence has a long tradition in Rio Arriba County, a beautiful, green part of New Mexico where most of the land is owned by the U.S. Forest Service (which leases much of it to lumber and cattle concerns) or by a few Anglo ranchers who hold enormous chunks of acreage.

The county is very poor. It has a high rate of infant mortality, and of its 27,000 inhabitants, 35 percent live below the poverty level. About 82 percent have Spanish surnames.

The center of Tierra Amarilla, which is the county seat of Rio Arriba, is a dusty, dirt-road intersection. All the frame buildings are boarded up and obviously not in use. Huddled together on a nearby small hill are about sixty houses, most of them tiny and with tin roofs. It is on this hill that the people live. Dogs, goats, and sheep roam free in the yards on the hill and even down on the deserted main corner of the town.

It's deserted except for a sheriff's car, which is parked

before a mind-boggling display of political power—a huge, beige birthday cake of a building with columns and balustrades and ornately carved stone balconies that overlook the empty corner. This is the county courthouse and it houses the Sheriff's Department of Rio Arriba County. The building is both the symbol and actual site of the violence that has rocked this part of the Southwest for the past fifteen years.

We arrived in T.A., as it is called, at dusk and wanted to take a picture of the building. As we were photographing, a battered old pickup truck wheeled into our camera range and stopped. A cowboy-hatted man leaned his head out and said, "You can't do that. You can't take pictures of the sheriff's building here; it is not allowed." He waited until we moved on.

On June 5, 1967, pictures of this building were in every major newspaper and magazine in the country. The dirt road was surrounded by National Guardsmen and armored tanks a few hours after the courthouse had been riddled with bullets by a militant Chicano group, the *Alianza de los Pueblos Libres* (Alliance of Free City-States). They had tried to make a citizens' arrest of the district attorney, who was in the court- house. The group's leader, Reies Lopez Tijerina, was brought to trial on charges of assault to commit murder at what has since been called the Courthouse Raid. His bodyguard and driver at the time was nineteen- year-old Moises Morales. After a search of the nearby mountains by police in helicopters and tanks, Morales was also brought in and thrown in jail for his role in the raid.

Today, Morales is thirty-one and running for sheriff of Rio Arriba on the La Raza Unida party slate (a third political party, whose name means The Race— referring to Spanish-speaking peoples—United). He still looks as if he has just come out of hiding in those mountains. He is tall and very thin, with dark, almost black hair. You don't realize how tight and hunched over people's shoulders can be until you see somebody like Morales, who is so relaxed. He is quiet and speaks with some hesitation. He has a Spanish accent and chooses his words carefully, seeming to want to find the precise, right way of saying something. But he has no trouble understanding what others say, even when they speak in the most colloquial English. He uses his hands to make what he says clearer, and you notice the hands because they're long and graceful—they are not the stubby-fingered scarred hands you might expect to find on a mechanic, which is what Morales is.

Moises Morales is not a Sixties radical turned Seventies in-the-system politician. The established political system in Rio Arriba County is as offended by his running for office today as it was by his part in the armed revolt twelve years ago. When Morales first ran for sheriff a few years ago, the political machine framed him.

Tierra Amarilla is Morales's home town. He has not come here to apply political theories learned someplace else or to organize a grass-roots movement. He is a revolutionary. He works and lives with a small group in T.A. that, ever since the Courthouse Raid, has joined together communally. Its entire effort is predicated on a close-knit group of people working in solidarity. Even the local press has trouble figuring out who is the head, or chief, of this political party.

Morales says, "They define me as a leader, the leader of La Raza Unida party. That's what they say, but I don't consider myself a leader because I don't believe in leaders. There's got to be those who go out and talk to people. If I'm campaigning and I don't have enough money for gas, I'll just hitch a ride. But I am campaigning still. A lot of people are doing it, especially the young people. There are a lot of young people who are tired of seeing what's going on in this country."

Under the umbrella of a project called *La Cooperacion*, Morales and his friends run an agricultural cooperative that anyone may join to farm and get food; and a successful medical facility, *La Clinica*, which serves the entire county, many of whose residents had no medical care at all before *La Clinica*'s opening in 1969. The clinic has been burned down once, set on fire intentionally. Rebuilt, it and the cooperative are today, a collection of aluminum-roofed makeshift structures. Behind the clinic is a small garage, where Moises Morales works as a mechanic.

"I have my shop out there and I meet a lot of people there. Outsiders come, and I check their cars, and they ask about the history of Rio Arriba, and I tell them about the history. And the first thing they see is a picture of me in the back of my truck, and it says, 'Morales for Sheriff, La Raza Unida. So they ask, 'Aren't you that guy?' and I say, 'Yeah.' And I give them a little story why I got involved."

Morales earns his living as a mechanic, but mostly he brings in money to help finance the group's other projects. These include a law office that provides government food stamps and gives assistance to anyone and, most recently, a welfare rights program.

This sense of commitment to "the people" and to a communal sharing of resources sets Morales's campaign apart from others in the United States. In fact, it is not *his* campaign; it is *their* (and that means everyone's) campaign. The issues in Rio Arriba County are basic—gut changes must be made in the way people live—so that every action taken by this group is tied to every other move they make. To young people like *La Clinica*'s receptionist and the male nurse we met the night we interviewed Morales, the political campaign is interwoven with the work of the clinic and also with their efforts in the agricultural coop and welfare organization. They talk about their work with the same sense of "we're all in this together" you hear in other campaigns, but they are talking about deeper changes to be made and have more deeply held views about land and people. We asked Morales if he would use the word "Marxist" to describe himself.

"Well," he said, "I could say it was irrelevant, but"—he smiled and rubbed his hair, pausing—"I don't know. I define myself 'cause I want justice. I mean for everybody, not just for Chicanos. I want it for a lot of people, because the way I see it is that if people don't start sticking together, something is going to happen. People are tired of being harassed by the rich. It's not just here; it's all over the world."

There's no way to even begin to make sense out of the politics of this part of the Southwest without first knowing about land. Land and who owns it is the basic issue around which the *Alianza* was formed; it was the question on which the La Raza Unida party first organized, and it is the key factor in Morales's commitment to politics.

"Since I was small," he says, "I always knew about the land grants. My grandfather had a house in the San Joaquin land grant, which he built. He and my grandmother had their sheep, cows, and bulls. My grandfather told me lots of stories about the land grants. When the old people would get together, they'd talk about it, when the land was free and they had horses and all kinds of sheep."

Most of the land in New Mexico was originally part of Mexico. In the early 1800's, the Mexican government made out large land grants to individual citizens and entire communities of people. Many of these grants, though assigned to individuals, had really been held by communities, called *Los Pueblos*. The pueblos decided which part of the land grant would be used for which purposes (in much the same way that the original Pilgrims divided up Plymouth Plantation), and all community members were allowed to graze or farm these parcels communally.

When the United States won this territory from Mexico in 1848, it promised in the Treaty of Guadalupe Hidalgo to honor and protect the land rights of the Spanish people living in the territory. But U.S. law has no history of recognizing communal ownership and use, and so the pueblos' deeds were deemed "vague" and "extralegal" by American Courts of Public Land Claims.

"The rich people started coming," Morales says, "and they started fencing the lands or buying them up very cheaply. These were not only outsiders, but people inside, too—our own people who kept a little bit ahead of all the other people. And people like my grandfather—well, he couldn't understand."

Almost all the land that didn't fall into private hands became part of the public domain. Then, in the early 1900's, Theodore Roosevelt's dreams of conservation sped the creation of a national forest service, and millions of acres of public land were given over to it. Contrary to what most people think, U.S. Forest Service lands are not like national parks, used exclusively for recreation and conservation. Often, the Forest Service leases out land to large lumber companies, ranching operations, and other private entrepreneurs. Thousands of acres of the old Tierra Amarilla land grant are now part of the Carson National Forest, and it is the Forest Service that gets to decide who may use the land and for what purpose.

Morales never sounds angrier than when he describes what happened after the Forest Service closed off the land to the small farmers and herders who had been using it for grazing, wood, and fishing. "Suddenly," he says, "in order to keep the cattle in the forest, you had to have permits. So first they [the Forest Service] grabbed the milk cows; then they took the saddle horses; and then they started taking from your other herds so you couldn't get any money for them, for the other cows. My grandfather kept on sending letters to all the politicians, and all they'd say was, 'We'll look into it; we've got a lot of other work to do.' That's when I really started getting involved in politics. I said to myself, 'When I get big, I'm going to at least try to straighten the problem out.'

"I used to go to rallies with my grandfather— Democratic meetings at the range hall—and they'd promise everything, get them all drunk and give them promises, right before the primaries: 'I'm gonna fix your road, give you cow permits,' you know, any problem you had. And then the primary would come, and after it, it'd be the same old shit. They'd promise anything."

"Return the land grants" has been a rallying cry to militant Chicanos in this area for over a hundred years. Immediately after the Civil War, Spanish leaders organized for restoration; and around 1912, the famed *Mano Negra* (Black Hand) rode through the area destroying Forest Service fences and burning down fields. In the mid-1960's, Chicano power emerged on the heels of black power, and in this part of the Southwest it focused on the question of the land grants. The leader of the movement was a short, stocky, and charismatic ex-preacher, the son of a sharecropper, Reies Tijerina. At first, the demonstrations were peaceful: long, quiet marches through the county to the governor's office in Albuquerque; assemblies and rallies and small meetings. Moises Morales, at this time, was living away from home, working as a sheepherder on a ranch in Utah.

"I was in the desert," he recalls. "I had on the radio, and I could hear this guy talking about the land grants. So I couldn't take it anymore." He came back to Tierra Amarilla and joined Tijerina's band. At eighteen, known for being a skilled driver with a good knowledge of the state's back roads, Morales became Tijerina's driver and bodyguard. At the time Morales joined them, Tijerina and his supporters were being harassed constantly by officials. Tijerina was jailed or detained several times on trumped-up charges; his people were picked up and interrogated by local police, who tried to stop the *Alianza* from meeting or giving speeches. Morales's job was to circumvent these attempts, by moving Tijerina freely and safely around the state.

"I had a real fast car then, and nobody could keep up. I could get him through the county in four hours. And I used to go to Albuquerque to take him to speak at those colleges. And along the way we would change cars about ten times. People would be following us."

The people who followed them were usually the state police or U.S. marshal and longtime political boss, Emilio Naranjo. By June, 1967, police were interrogating and arresting residents, in anticipation of an *Alianza* meeting called by Tijerina. Those brought in by the police were suspected of being *Alianza* members or supporters.

"We were going to have a big meeting," says Morales, "so they started arresting people the day before the meeting. We decided to make a citizens' arrest ourselves of the district attorney for denying us freedom of assembly and freedom of speech; we were going to arrest him and take him to the state attorney general's office. And when you make a citizen's arrest you can use any force you need."

Tijerina's group shot up the county courthouse, seized control of it for an hour and a half, then escaped holding two hostages. It was then that the governor called in the National Guard and its tanks, and after a manhunt that went on for several days, Morales was one of the last to be brought in.

"I was on top of a rock hiding in the country, and they were looking for me with helicopters. It was a lot of publicity, and for years after, people were afraid of me; it's hard to watch tanks coming into your town. It's like a world war."

Tijerina was jailed briefly, and did not return to T.A. Shortly after the raid, Moises split from Tijerina and worked in T.A. with some of the families who had been in the *Alianza* to set up the clinic and coop that are there today. The land grants remained the most important issue.

"Politics involves all kinds of things, and I think the land grants must be shared. I mean shared among each other 'cause the people here would much rather be self-supporting. Right now sixty percent of the people are on welfare and food stamps and all that, but when they had their land grants, they had all they wanted. They had beef, they had wood—now, you can't even go for wood. If they catch you cutting illegally, they send you to jail; if you go for wood in the forest here, you gotta take out a permit to get wood. So one of my issues here is the land grants. But you've got to get the people real organized first."

The group decided to organize into a third political party, calling it the La Raza Unida party. They felt that neither the Democrats (who control the county) nor the Republicans were about to make any changes: "The Republicans have never done anything to help the people; they just steal. They make deals with the party in power. So let's say La Raza Unida was not on the ballot, and we let the Democrats and the Republicans compete. It would be the same thing all over again. They won't change anything. It's got to be younger people, another party, to change it—because all there is, is the people."

In 1975 Morales ran for sheriff on the La Raza slate. The issue that made him decide to do it was police brutality, particularly against those who supported the coop and the clinic.

"They were catching people and knocking the shit out of them," he recalls. "Pregnant women—they would kick them; one had a miscarriage."

The main thrust of La Raza's campaign that year was against the corruption of county officials, controlled by Naranjo, by now a county commissioner, who had further tightened his hold on Rio Arriba finances.

"They misuse the county's funds," charges Morales, "the taxpayers' money. Like they buy thousands of dollars in road equipment each year, and the roads never change. They buy equipment for eighty thousand dollars that's only worth forty thousand dollars; then they get all that kickback. They use it for campaigns."

In the middle of his campaign for sheriff, Morales was stopped in his car by deputies one night as he was driving home. They tied up his hands and asked him to "walk the line." At this moment, Morales's brother drove by, and Moises shouted to him to go home and tell people what was happening. When it became clear that the deputies couldn't detain Morales for drunken driving, he saw one of the deputies put something in his truck. It turned out to be marijuana, in quantities large enough to justify jailing him. He was brought to the county jail to be held for trial. Morales says it could have been much worse.

Though La Raza and Morales lost that election, the marijuana bust turned out to help their cause. At Morales's trial in criminal court for possession of marijuana, wildly illegal practices in the Sheriff's Department came to light, including two county officers' admission that dope planting by police was a common means of dealing with political opponents. Moises Morales was acquitted, and went on to receive—in a subsequent civil suit in which he charged

that he was framed by, among others, Naranjo—a
$10,000 out-of-court settlement. Naranjo and one of
his deputies (the present sheriff of Rio Arriba) were
convicted for perjury resulting from that trial.

"All that opened the people's eyes," says Morales.
"In the few years since La Raza was formed, we've
accomplished a lot. We have brought all the corruption out to the people. All the work that I do, I do on
top of the table. We're not hiding anything. Every
time there's an issue that's going to hurt the people,
we're right there before the county commissioners. We
tell them our position, what we want, and what is
wrong. They said there wasn't any corruption in the
county government, and it turned out that they had to
pay me $10,000 damages for my frame-up.

"I knew I wasn't going to get elected the first time,
but after going through all the shit that I had gone
through, I decided that I was going to show Naranjo
that I wasn't afraid, like the Republicans who had
opposed him for the past twenty years. They hadn't
done in twenty years what we had done in two years.
We could confront him. We'd just go out and tell him
what he was; we weren't afraid or anything. The night
of the election, when the ballots were coming in, we
had my truck full of beer in the back, and we were
drinking the beer in front of the courthouse. And when
I passed the 1000-vote mark (Morales lost with 1300
votes; the Republican candidate had over 2000, and

the Democrat 4000), I went up to the deputy and said, 'Hey, man, you want to fight?' and they asked me why. I said, 'Because you guys planted the marijuana on me, that's why.' And they were all chicken; they were crazy."

It's apparent as you talk to Morales and the people he works with that the possibility of violence against them, their families, and the places in which they work is something they live with constantly. The clinic has been burned down, and Moises and others have been shot at. "Sometimes I have fear that I might get shot, by snipers, from behind," he says. "If I get elected and do the job of straightening out the Sheriff's Department, there might be people wanting to kill me for that, on their side, to get rid of me.

"If I'm ever sheriff, I'm not going to work like the last sheriffs we've had in this county. I'm not going to bust people for marijuana and things like that. I think there's a whole group of things that messing around with costs the taxpayers more money, when there's bigger things going on in this county, like murders—and heroin. I'm against that. But on marijuana, I'll tell people, 'Don't go shine it in my face just because I'm agreeing with you, because then I'll do it.' But I'm not going to mess around with that. I mean, ninety percent of the people I know smoke marijuana. Everybody smokes it, I guess. I don't; but I'm not against it. That was one of the biggest mistakes that they made when they planted the marijuana on me, because everybody knew that I didn't smoke marijuana."

Listening to Morales, it seems easier to say what the things are that he *won't* do as sheriff. After all, the people in Rio Arriba have had over twenty years of examples of what not to do in the job. Running against corruption and against police brutality goes down well with most people, except perhaps those in power in the county. What's more difficult is to explain to the people what *should* be done, what Morales and the others will fight for if they win. In the end, as always in Rio Arriba, it comes down to the land and its ownership. On this point, Morales and La Raza do not waver one bit.

"What could be done to improve the people's living conditions here is, number one, always the land and the land grants. It's hard. A lot of people say that if the land grants come down, that's when the war is going to start. Some people are going to say, 'Well, we've been here more than you, you know, we should have more than you.' So it's a hard question. But I think there are ways. For one thing, if we get the land grants out, by that time the people are going to be organized, because that's the only way we're going to get the land grants out. The people have got to be organized for that. And if you have them organized to get the land grants out, then you'll have them organized to share the land.

"People have to get their lands back, to have them

cooperatively again, where everybody can survive, not that each one gets his own land back. I'm not saying, 'This one gets one thousand cows, and this one gets one cow.' It should all be controlled. Everybody should take just what they need."

Nancy Stevenson

☆

"They Want Their Women Ladylike in This State"

The typical woman political candidate is married, has grown children, and is forty-six years or older. She is also white, Protestant, and although she has been active in party politics, has never held public office. Nancy Stevenson, the new lieutenant-governor of South Carolina, is most of these things, but she won in a state that had never before elected a woman to a major statewide office. According to a poll taken of women candidates, those in the East and West felt that being a woman helped their campaigns; those in the South and Midwest thought their sex was a handicap.

South Carolina was the state that "started" the Civil War. The newly organized Confederate government's order for the firing on Fort Sumter, a federal fort that was built on a sandbar in the harbor of Charleston, was the opening shot of that four-year tragedy. A state that had thrived on cotton, indigo, rice, and slavery—the last deemed essential to continue the other three—

South Carolina also had the largest black population of any southern state.

After the Civil War, blacks took advantage of Reconstruction to elect a black majority to both their new state constitutional convention and to the legislature. They wrote the most progressive laws the state had ever known, inaugurating a new public school system, reforming local government, abolishing imprisonment for debt, and extending the vote to all free men, even allowing for the reinstatement of Confederates.

In the 1880's, when white Democrats regained control, they tried to make sure black power would never happen again. They kept almost all of the other reforms, but blacks were deprived of all political, economic, and social rights.

South Carolina stagnated economically from that time on, and for most of this century the state has had one of the lowest per capita incomes in the United States, as well as an astonishingly low level of state aid to educational and health services. In spite of heavy investment in the state by defense industries, South Carolina today is not really a part of the new economic South. It relies heavily on textile manufacturing that needs cheap, unskilled labor in order to make profits.

Politically it is a Democratic state, although perhaps the least so of the southern states. Its people have voted for the Republican candidate in three of the past four presidential elections and, given the opportunity, have shown their willingness to vote for right-wing politicians. Nancy Stevenson is a liberal Democrat.

You hear the full description of her: that she is pro-ERA in a state that has refused to ratify the Equal Rights Amendment; she is against the death penalty in a state that has people on Death Row awaiting execution. The Women's Campaign Fund, an organization that supports women's candidacies, called her campaign an "essential and important one" and helped it to the tune of $5000; and she has been attacked in the primary for (1) being an "outsider" and (2) having written a "racy" novel in which she referred to a few South Carolinians as "culture-starved, tater-poppin', egg-suckin' rednecks." If this conjures up an image of an outspoken, hard-edged activist, that image is quickly dispelled when you lay eyes on Nancy Stevenson.

She is gracious and charming, a fifty-year-old woman who shares in the southern tradition of political cunning and love of maneuvering that continues to dominate national politics. She is not an outsider. Although born in New York, her mother came from an old (that's three centuries old) Charleston family. Stevenson currently lives on a street in Charleston named after her family.

She went into politics as a result of her work in community affairs. She had spent much time organizing tutorial programs for children and was deeply involved in Charleston historic-restoration projects. But she considers her first political act to have been filing for election to the state's House of Representatives four years ago. Before that, "I'd never been to a precinct meeting; I'd never done anything. I had helped my husband, who ran for the Assembly and had served for three years. And then he didn't run again. Sixteen years elapsed."

In 1974 Nancy Stevenson was elected to the state's House of Representatives, the lower house of the legislature. There are 124 members in the House, and most of them are Democrats. Each House member represents about 20,000 people. Members receive $7000 per year (plus an expense allowance of $25 per day when the House is in session) plus travel and postage allowances. By state government standards, this is one of the lowest payment rates in the country. A representative is not in a position of great power, but that did not thwart Stevenson's interests or plans. Within two years, a major bill she had sponsored passed by an unheard-of unanimous vote. Stevenson describes what happened:

"I had wanted to find money for human services, specifically to reduce the teacher-pupil ratio in our public schools. Everybody kept saying, 'You know, we've got plenty of money, all you have to do is cut out the fat in state government.' So I started out looking for the fat. And I discovered to my absolute horror that we had no way of knowing what we did with our tax dollars once we had given them away to the various arms of state government. I couldn't believe it! How can you run anything—even a household budget—if you don't know what you spend your money on? So I put in a bill, called the Fiscal Accountability Bill, which required uniform quarterly reports of all state expenditures. And the agencies did not take kindly to this."

Stevenson began a one-person campaign to have her bill become law before the institutional groups and lobbies could gather their forces and oppose the legislation.

"I started off by selling the concept to my colleagues. I called over half the House during the summer, and they went along with the concept. Then I kept sending them drafts and asking for their comments. Then I'd call them up to see if they had any comments. Many of them, I think, had never even read the draft and therefore they would say, 'No, it looks great.'"

She also campaigned with the press. "The news media took it up and wrote about forty very favorable editorials, all around the state, in every paper you could find. They began pushing for this thing, so it became sort of like motherhood and apple pie. The press was very helpful on this, to the point where I went to one of the senators and said, 'I hope you're going to support this bill,' and he said, 'Nancy, where I come from, it would be political suicide to vote against that bill.'

"I think the agencies themselves did not take much interest in the beginning, because they thought, 'Oh, well, that's a freshman female member. No way—forget it. We've got other things to worry about.' And then, lo and behold, it passed the House, 101 to 0."

The Speaker of the House, who had served for over twenty years, said it was the only time in his memory that any major legislation had passed unanimously. Stevenson made her name on the legislation—it was soon dubbed the Stevenson Act—and, as she says, "had I not done that, I would never be lieutenant-governor now."

Nancy Stevenson's campaign for lieutenant-governor began in January 1978. It was a three-way race for the Democratic nomination: herself and two Senators Smith. "At first, everybody greeted the news of my candidacy with 'How nice. Who else is running?' and it was very difficult to get the public to take me seriously and to convince them that I was competent. People *assume* that male candidates are competent; but they do not make that assumption with female candidates. I'd say between seventy and seventy-five percent of my advertising was addressed to the proof of my competency. Most of the people didn't think I could win until they woke up the morning after the first primary."

In South Carolina, if no candidate in a race for statewide office wins 50 percent of the vote, a runoff is held between the top two vote-getters. Horace Smith, a twelve-year veteran of the state legislature, emerged from the primary as Stevenson's opponent in the September runoff.

"It was a dirty campaign," she says. "My husband had been warning me all along: 'Wait for the last-minute tactic.'" First she was attacked for being an "outsider." But though born in New York, Nancy Stevenson is as Carolinian as they come. "I was born in New Rochelle, and I lived there for nine months or something. Then we moved to Manhattan. But my father, who was a New Yorker, died when I was four, and my mother, who was a South Carolinian, did not thrive up in Yankeeland, and she came home. So. . . . I don't know as when you went around Charleston, you might have driven down Legare Street. Well, my mother was a Legare. Her family had come over in, what, 1693 or something.

"My opponent tried to say I wasn't from South Carolina, but in point of fact he was thirty-nine, and I figured out I had lived in South Carolina more than he ever had, because I'd lived here for forty years. He hadn't been here as long as I had."

Senator Smith's next line of attack was on a book she had coauthored. Under various pen names Stevenson had written three novels, the most recent of which was *Savage Summer*, a modern romance set in South Carolina. Senator Smith stumped the state with a copy of the book, saying that because Stevenson wrote it, she was of "questionable moral fiber." The attack backfired, though, and may have actually helped Stevenson's campaign.

"South Carolinians are a very decent people, and they do not like personal attacks. It's a bad enough no-no to attack a man; but the real no-no is to attack a woman. It isn't done. It's partly because the state is as chauvinistic as it is, I think, that the reaction was as strong as it was. Men who never would have considered voting for me voted for me out of anger over what was done to me.

"He was terribly foolish, too, because the press asked him, 'What specifically was so terrible about the book?' and he hadn't actually read it. Well, to question somebody's moral character having never read the book is a little—well—questionable. And really, as my brother says—he says, 'Nanny, the only thing bad about your book is that it's boring.' Which is a very unkind cut!"

Other issues separated her from Senator Smith, and these were used in the campaign. In many states the code words "abortion" and "death penalty" can signal the start of large political fights, with the pro's and the anti's marshaling huge, sometimes irrational, forces—not so much to elect a particular candidate who shares their views but, more often, to *defeat* one who doesn't. In South Carolina, one must add the Equal Rights Amendment as an issue that resembles waving a red flag. South Carolina refused to ratify the ERA. Nancy Stevenson had been a co-sponsor of the ratification bill, which was defeated under the leadership of Senator Smith. "He then tried to make it into an issue in the campaign, saying, oh, you know, 'She's against home and family,' and yuk, yuk, yuk. But it never worked, since ERA's chance of being passed was always slim.

"Abortion, too, couldn't materialize as a crucial issue [Stevenson takes the women's rights position on that issue], since there was nothing in the hopper. We have abortions in this state but, best I know, they are not federally funded unless it's for rape or incest. So it's not an issue in that sense.

"And that goes for the death penalty as well. They fussed with me because I voted against the death penalty. But that really isn't an issue either, because although I voted against it, it passed. It's hard to create a campaign issue out of something that was successful, even though I opposed it. People would want to know 'Why did you oppose the death penalty?' and I had two reasons. I opposed it because I do not feel it is a deterrent. I personally supported and worked for and fought for—on the floor of the House—an amendment which would have changed the death penalty to life imprisonment with no parole. I think that's a *real* deterrent. I also opposed it because if you look at the history of this state, no one has ever been executed in South Carolina unless they've been poor, be they white or black. Well, I just said those things. You know, I had a real reason; and when you have a real reason, I find that even if people disagree with you, they can't get hot and bothered about it."

Nancy Stevenson makes it sound so easy. She was able to take positions on issues that defeat other candidates throughout the country (both male and female) and somehow turn them into nonissues. She meanwhile used her campaign to talk about state finances, economics, and education—issues *she* wanted to see discussed. She got away with it. She seems to have always been in complete control of the campaign and the image she was projecting to the voters. She has that rare combination of intelligence, clarity in the way she explains issues and herself, plus a streak of horse sense that tells her when to duck and when to come out fighting (always with gentility).

She says she thinks she got away with this in part because of her age. "In my case, being a little long in the tooth, being fifty, and having grown up in a—I would say a more polite era—people in this state could accept me on a basis that they couldn't have accepted a younger person, a younger woman. I would go into an old filling station, let's say, and I would say, 'I'm Nancy Stevenson. I'm running for lieutenant-governor.' And they'd say, 'Miss Nancy, oh, I saw you on television, come on in and sit down and have a—' I was 'Miss Nancy' to half of South Carolina. And that was kinda nice. But obviously if I had been thirty instead of fifty, I wouldn't have been 'Miss Nancy' to half of South Carolina."

It's pretty hard to call Nancy Stevenson "long in the tooth." She's a young-looking fifty by any account, and she exudes energy and humor that seem to be saying, "See, I can do anything if I put my mind to it." She would be "easy to package" in any political campaign. And she is sophisticated enough to realize that she had to have the best packaging in order to win.

"I didn't do any more media than either of my opponents, but it was better media, because it was written by one of the best people in the business, the creative director of McCann Erickson [one of the largest ad agencies in the world], who just happens to be my brother. He wrote it for me, and it was really tops! Just super! And he didn't say anything that I hadn't actually done. I had created the stuff for him to use. *I'd* done that. My service had done that. I don't think either of the Senators Smith had similar accomplishments to point to, you see. But it had to be pointed to and done right. It's not easy in thirty seconds.

"The ads were simple. They were really very unassuming. One of them was in front of the statehouse, and I said, 'I'm not part of the Old Boy political network. Obviously, I never will be. I'm Nancy Stevenson, and I'm running for lieutenant-governor. As a legislator, I wrote the first fiscal accountability act in the history of this state. It brought bureaucratic spending out in the open, and the papers named it the Stevenson Act. It wasn't an act of genius, just an act of independence.'"

As she recited this ad verbatim—it just rolled out without our having asked—her eyes focused on something beyond the room, perhaps on an imagined TV camera. It was as if we had disappeared. Yet we're sure that when South Carolinians saw the ad on their TV screens, what came across was a direct, sincere, straight look in the eye. Like good actors, politicians who know how to use media are able to create this earnest look at the drop of a hat. You realize that they've practiced how they look when they speak— maybe by watching themselves speak at home, say, sitting across from a mirror at dinner. They know how their eyes focus, how their hands gesticulate. They know how they're coming across.

Stevenson's whole family helped. She calls her

brother "the crucial factor in my victory, the secret up my sleeve," but her daughter, Farraday, turned out to be a political asset too. "She took a semester out of college and traveled with me from January through August. She was my driver, my body person, the person with whom we got lost. But it was great having her. It was great to have that time together, and it was also politically terribly beneficial. One of the big questions people have about women candidates is, 'Are you leaving little children at home?' Well, there was my twenty-one-year-old daughter, and it showed that my children were grown. They're seventeen, twenty, twenty-one, and twenty-seven, so, you know, I'm not leaving little people. Also, people wonder if your family is behind you. Well, if your daughter's right there with you, obviously that answers that question. Those are two big questions.

"It was funny, though, when the book thing came up, my daughter, little Farraday, got so mad at Senator Horace Smith that if she saw him, she would walk across the street. She would not speak to him. The whole thing didn't trouble me the way it troubled her. And then she said, 'Mama, which would make you madder: if somebody cut you down, or if they cut Uncle Bill down?' And I said, 'They can cut me down all they want, but I'd kill them if they cut down my brother!' And she said, 'Well, that's the way I feel when they cut you down.' Farraday probably will never forget. But it's all gone to me. I'm going on to something else."

Stevenson has given up writing for the time being. The "something else" is clearly politics, and probably higher office. At first, when we asked her to explain why she is drawn to both writing and politics, she said she saw no connection between the two. Later, after she thought about it, she said decisively, "I *can* make a correlation. They are both very creative. Coming up with the most direct, most practical solutions to problems takes a great deal of ingenuity and creativity. First, to see the core of the problem, not the periphery; to treat the disease and not the symptoms; and to come up with the proper cure for the disease. I think that takes a lot of creativity. There are so many ways to skin a cat. To try one way, and if that way is blocked, to come up with another. Can you see that politics would be very challenging?"

It is said of many state legislators in this country that if they're not corrupt, they're inept. It's also said that at best most of them react; they are not real initiators of change either because of lack of staff and money or the fact that for many it's just a part-time job. Stevenson agrees, saying, "A lot of it is the part-time job. You know, they can barely keep on top of all the legislation coming down the pike. And so most legislation is just knee-jerk reaction to some crisis or someone else's interest. But I haven't approached politics that way. I am sought out by the same lobbying groups as the others, but as a female legislator—most of us do not run businesses or have professions, so there's not a great deal that the lobbyist has to offer. They could have bought thousands of copies of my book, and it wouldn't have made much difference to me!

"I hate generalizations, but I will make one: people perceive that women in politics are less bribeable, rightly or wrongly. What I do find, though, is that, generally speaking, a larger percentage of female legislators vote on the basis of reason than do male legislators. I mean, if you approach one of these female legislators on the basis of sweet reason, she'll go with you. I also think women are—generally speaking here again, this is not true of all women and not true of all men, but generally speaking—they're less hung up on power. If they want power, they want it in order to accomplish what they want to accomplish, not for its own sake."

There is simply no way of knowing. Women in America have simply not had enough political power for anyone to know how they'll use it. For all Stevenson's accomplishment in winning the lieutenant-governorship, it's still a fact that the office has little power. Whereas the governor of South Carolina is paid $39,000 a year, and the secretary of state, comptroller general, attorney general, and state treasurer each receive $34,000 (those four offices are, in theory, *under* that of lieutenant-governor), Nancy Stevenson's new job pays a mere $16,250. In looking for subjects for our book, we ran into a number of women who were running for lieutenant-governor in various states. Several won, and these are noticeable achievements. But we also notice that the job is usually one of low pay and lower prestige; and it has no power. In other words, perhaps, it is "O.K. to give it to a woman," or to a minority-group member.

The area where being a woman was a handicap to Nancy Stevenson—as it is to almost all women candidates—was fund raising. In most political races, whether the polls show it or not, women candidates are at first presumed to "not stand a chance" of winning. A chance of winning is what makes people open up their checkbooks to your campaign. Women have had to rely on small contributions from friends and believers to put together their campaign chests. Although there is some evidence that this is changing, it's a slow process. At least one organization now operating on the national level—The Women's Campaign Fund— has as its major purpose the financial support of women's campaigns. The fund gave Nancy Stevenson $5000 in her race, and it was perhaps her largest single contribution.

"Oh, dear heavenly fathers! I have a debt that rivals the feds'. I'd ask organizations that usually give contributions to candidates, but they didn't think I would win, so I'd get the ten dollars, and my opponents would get the hundred dollars. We had fund raising committees and benefits; and my campaign manager sent my picture with a letter to NOW's [National Organization of Women] magazine and, do you know, we raised almost eighteen hundred dollars from women all over this country. They sent one dollar, fives, one check for two hundred, but mostly fives and twos or ones."

Of total campaign expenditures of $250,000, she was able to raise $100,000. She went into personal debt to the bank for the remaining $150,000. "The only thing I'm beholden to," she says, "is the bank. And if you can't go to the bank, you'd better not run if you're a female.

"If I had any advice to give to a female going into politics, I would say get involved in your community first. That proves to people that you care, and you will work, and you can produce. And should you have small children, stay on a local level in politics or, if you live close by the Capitol, then on a state level. Don't try to run for Washington with small children 'cause the voters won't elect you, unless you happen to have a husband who is a writer or something, who can move with you when you have to come to Washington. But if you don't, the voters won't go with that; and I can't say I blame them. If you wanted to leave kids, you shouldn't have had 'em, you know.

"I would also advise them to go through the ranks, in the sense of not trying immediately for a huge top slot. That doesn't mean you can't do it the other way, but it sure makes it tough to try and shoot for a top job without having served at all before.

"Each state is different for women candidates. You know, they want their women ladylike in this state. And feminine. And to do that and still be able to convince people that you can perform, that you can accomplish things, that you *are* credible, and are qualified, is very difficult."

Arthur Eve

"Give the Brothers and Sisters Some Role in the Struggle"

It would be pretty hard to turn down an appeal made by Arthur Eve personally. The assemblyman from Buffalo, New York, has that quality all politicians want and few have—charisma. As he speaks before a black political collective on the day we interviewed him, every face in the room is focused on him. It was an audience that includes mothers with infants in their arms and other politicians, who are notorious for not being able to focus on anybody but themselves.

Arthur Eve is a handsome man, tall and broad-shouldered, in his late forties. He moves well, with the natural grace of a good athlete. He has no nervous mannerisms; his hands are still except when he uses them to illustrate a point. He looks entirely comfortable—and he makes those around him feel comfortable.

By the middle of his speech, when he is really going full speed on the subject of black versus white politics, the audience is answering back with "Yea, man" and

"You are right, brother; tell 'em, brother." We are the
only white people in the room, but we don't feel out of
place. More than that, we want to get down to work
right away on the things Eve is speaking about.

Minority politics is increasingly a politics of separ-
ateness. The Democratic party coalition that has held
together for the last forty years—blacks, the unions,
and liberals—is gradually coming apart. Although a
serious third-party movement on either a national or a
state level has not yet developed, blacks, Chicanos,
Native Americans, and other groups that used to
identify with the Democratic party are now saying,
"Only by sticking together with our own will we have
any strength."

In 1977 Arthur Eve unexpectedly won the Democratic primary for mayor in Buffalo. An unprecedented
77 percent of eligible black voters cast their ballots. It
was only the third time in U.S. history that so high a
percentage of the black voters turned out. Eve received
95 percent of black votes. His opponent was the county
political machine's candidate. In the general election
Eve was defeated when the established Democratic
organization worked to undermine his candidacy. The
Conservative party's candidate ultimately won the
election.

Eve never thought about being a politician when he
grew up. Originally from Florida, he moved to Buffalo
in the 1950's, after an army stint in Germany. In Buffalo,

his first job was in a factory, but he had always been interested in kids and sports. "I was working in the Chevrolet plant that summer, and I saw kids playing dice games in the park. I saw recreational directors who would come, throw out the basketballs in the morning, then go to their other jobs. It really was a ripoff. I said to my wife, 'Gee, I'd like to work with kids in the summer. Can I take a leave from the factory and work with these kids?' It meant a cut in pay, but she agreed.

"I applied to the city for a recreational position, and the guy looked at my background—I'd been All-High in Florida for basketball, All-Europe in the army, and I'd run a program for orphans in the army in Germany. He said, 'What a fantastic background! But you've got to see your ward leader.'

"At the time I don't think I was a registered voter. But I found the ward leader. He concurred it was a good background but, he said, 'We save our jobs in the summer for our party loyals. This is our way of paying off people who have been loyal to the party and to the machine.' "

Eve had never seen anything like that down South. Being excluded from a job because he wasn't a party worker astounded him. "It was my first real involvement on a political question, and I found it appalling. I grew up in Florida, where in the summer time we had so many activities for kids—a Bible school pro-

gram in the morning; lunch; if you were poor, the
community provided breakfast; basketball, track, and
baseball teams; we had buses to pick us up from one
park and take us to another; swimming matches and
tennis. Leaving the South and coming to the great
North, I could not believe that kids would not have
something better than what we had. I said to my wife,
'I'd better get involved in politics, because politics
determines the quality of recreation for kids.' "

So Eve joined the party, got the job, and for one
year worked within an old-line Democratic club. By
1958 he was organizing his own insurgent group of
young Democrats, a group that would be open to all
blacks, including those who were newly registered by
the group. He became a ward leader, the only one in
Buffalo outside the control of the county Democratic
machine. Within a short time, he emerged as a
leading independent activist, radical in his work for
minority rights. In 1966 he ran for a seat in the state
assembly—and he won.

He recalls, "When I first ran, a lot of my friends
said, 'Hey, man, you're going into that system? It's no
good; it's racist; it's oppressive.' And I said, 'Hey, if I
can get in there and make that system responsive, I've
got an obligation to try. For me to stay on the outside
and just throw darts and not try to affect it from the
inside—I don't think I'd be doing what I ought to.' "

Eve's idea of working within the system means never

letting up on the pressure to make it better. Sometimes the pressure takes forms that are unacceptable to other politicians and voters. In Eve's case, this happened when he threatened to lie down in front of bulldozers at state construction sites.

The construction unions in New York have a history of racism. Blacks were not allowed into apprenticeship programs and thus could not get into the construction union and work on the high-paying construction jobs. Eve began his protests in the winter, before the construction season got under way.

"Governor Rockefeller came to Buffalo. We met with him, and I said, 'We will not permit any work to begin when the season opens up. You're going to have to run over me with a bulldozer.' The governor, realizing that I meant it, and knowing my history and the support we had in the community—from a number of whites, too, for whites were very supportive of us in that effort—made a decision to stop the construction. I think the success of that demonstration was because I was an assemblyman, instead of just a guy. For them to put *me* in jail . . ."

Construction was stopped for a full eleven months, after which the governor negotiated with black leaders to stop the protests by opening up the unions.

"He literally bought some of the major black groups from under me," says Eve. "I was very frustrated. The end result was we developed a union program, but it wasn't up to the level I thought it should have been. We now have two or three hundred black men who have journeymen's cards; and there are others who went through the program but couldn't pass the exam, and they now have some skills they can sell. But it has not been the program we wanted.

"Rockefeller—if you had a price, that was the one thing he found. He found what our people's prices were, and he got them to accept the contract that I thought was insufficient. They all came to me and said, 'We know that you're against it, but will you go along? Will you give us a chance to try it?' I guess at the time I felt beaten. Part of my thing was 'O.K., go ahead, goddamn it, if this is what you want.' "

In the Assembly, Eve made prison reform one of his main concerns. "In '68 or '69, I got involved in prisons literally at the invitation of an elderly woman who did not have any transportation to Attica State Prison." Attica is New York's maximum-security facility, a massive fortress holding over twenty-two hundred prisoners on a remote piece of land about a hundred miles from Buffalo. The prison originally had been planned to house sixteen hundred inmates. "This woman asked if I would take her out there to see her son. I had never been to a state prison before, and it was just devastating to see that big, monstrous wall, to go through all the locks. I saw then for the first time all those black inmates, and Hispanics, and all white guards. Then, I just got involved in it."

Eve introduced several pieces of legislation aimed at changing prison and sentencing policies. One was a bill that would require an inmate to come up for parole consideration every three years, no matter what his sentence had been. At present, an inmate is eligible for parole review after he has served one-third of his sentence.

"My suggestion was this: Why not every three years have the person come and see where they are, see if they've been rehabilitated, see how they've moved? Then if the parole review body feels that this person has progressed, he then, of course, could be considered for parole at that time."

The bill never made it out of committee in the Assembly. Eve says, "Their argument was, 'These are murderers. They ought to stay in for at least fifteen or twenty years.' But really the prison system has found that when you stay in prison for more than seven years, that's when you really begin a downward trend as a person. And we have found that if you dehumanize a person and take him through a prison system which is not rehabilitative but really creates more animosity, hostility, and hatred, then that person you are letting out is really worse than what he was before he went in. And in the final analysis, if that person has not been 'rehabbed' or helped sufficiently, then you let out into society somebody who will ultimately commit a crime again, and maybe an even more vicious one. So the idea I had was, Why don't we set up a system where men who want to try to rehabilitate themselves can get themselves into good shape, because there will be a basic incentive—every three years they will have an opportunity for possible review."

Prison reform is not a popular issue. Nobody wins an election on it. A legislator who makes it a major concern gets mostly criticism from his constituents and endless mail appeals from prisoners and their families. Eve became "the man" in the legislature to send appeals to, and his office has been swamped with prisoner pleas and complaints since he introduced the parole review bill.

In September 1971 Attica exploded. Prisoners took over the facility, holding fifty guards as hostages. Eve knew firsthand many of the conditions the inmates were protesting. He had been there. He had seen the overcrowding, two and three men locked up in tiny cells: there was neither room nor time for physical exercising and no opportunity to participate in educational or rehabilitative programs; and Eve had heard many accounts of beatings inflicted on prisoners by guards (this was the chief complaint voiced by the men who took over Attica). Many prisoners knew Eve, and some had written to him. They accepted him as someone who might be on their side.

As soon as he heard about the riot, Eve went directly to the prison without being asked. The inmates' first demand was that Governor Rockefeller grant them amnesty for holding hostages. Eve walked into the prison's D yard, where he encountered twelve hundred inmates on the verge of violent upheaval.

"I thought it was a very critical and dangerous situation," he says. "I got into confrontations with some of them in the yard, but I thought somebody had to go in and start some dialogue. If the governor had only come and talked, not in the yard, but just talked through the phone, and guaranteed the inmates that they would not be beaten. That was the only thing the inmates wanted; that they would not be beaten, brutalized, or killed once the guards took over the facility again. That's all we asked Rockefeller to do, not even to go into the prison. And he refused to come. And what he did was to send in a massive force."

Even up to a minute before the attack on Monday morning, September 13, Eve thought Rockefeller would make some move toward negotiations. He watched with horror as troops surrounded D yard. He and others on the observer-negotiator committee pleaded with Rockefeller to do something to avoid a massacre. Eve had spent the previous night with sixteen other observers barricaded in the steward's room, part of the prison administration's office. Now, as he heard gunfire and saw gas beginning to seep around the window frames into the room in which they were locked, he sat imagining what was going on outside. It was the most emotionally draining time of his life.

Another observer, *New York Times* reporter Tom Wicker, wrote: "Eve was a profoundly shaken and disturbed man. He more and more saw himself as one of the D-yard brothers, a prisoner as much as they, whose life experience had pulled him steadily into their emotional orbit and whose sense of what was going to happen had brought him to something like despair."*

The massacre in D yard was as bad as Eve had imagined it would be. An attack force of two hundred state troopers (police and National Guardsmen later came in), armed with rifles and submachine guns and wearing gas masks, drowned the prison yard in rifle fire, then gas. The prisoners, armed only with knives and sticks, gave up. Forty-three people were killed: nine hostages; thirty-one prisoners; and three other people including a guard who died from injuries suffered during the revolt. The hostages were killed by gunfire from state police, not by the inmates. The prisoners' request to Rockefeller—that they be protected from further physical reprisals by guards once the revolt ended—was not granted. After the prisoners

*Tom Wicker, A *Time To Die* (New York: Quadrangle/New York Times Book Co., 1975), p. 240.

surrendered and the state regained control of Attica,
inmates tried to get court protection against further
beatings. Prisoners and one National Guardsman
testified before a federal district court:

> . . . beginning immediately after the State's recapture
> of Attica on the morning of September 13 and continu-
> ing at least until September 16, guards, state troopers and
> correctional personnel had engaged in cruel and inhu-
> man abuse of numerous inmates. Injured prisoners,
> some on stretchers, were struck, prodded or beaten with
> sticks, belts, bats or other weapons. Others were forced to
> strip and run naked through gauntlets of guards armed
> with clubs which they used to strike the bodies of the
> inmates as they passed. Some were dragged on the
> ground, some marked with an "X" on their backs, some
> spat upon or burned with matches, and others poked in
> the genitals or arms with sticks. According to the
> testimony of the inmates, bloody or wounded inmates
> were apparently not spared in this orgy of brutality."*

Eve came out of Attica with many of his beliefs
shattered. He had never thought that any government
within the United States could be that brutal. He told us
that for many nights after Attica, he would get on his
knees and pray (Eve is a religious man, a deacon of his
church), asking God how it could have happened

*Gonzalez v. Rockefeller, 10 Criminal Law Reporter 2227 (2d Cir., Dec. 1, 1971),
in Ronald L. Goldfarb and Linda R. Singer, After Conviction (New York:
Touchstone Books, 1973), p. 384.

and how man could treat his fellow man so inhumane-
ly. Eve emerged from this rough period resolved to use
whatever political power and skills he could muster to
force change, first by consolidating the power of his
own people. As you listen to him describe those days,
you realize it was then, at Attica, that Eve began to
sense that racism was a mainstay of white America in
the Seventies. The system was going to change only if
blacks organized themselves to change it.

Since that time, Eve has devoted his life to defining
and building up black power. He says, "It's important
that we know our strength and where we are. A lot of
times a lot of us try to influence the white political
system or the whole political system, and we do it from
emotions. That doesn't work any more. Emotional
response to a conservative, organized, reactionary
political system that exists in New York State today,
and throughout this country, does not get any response
from anybody. So you have to do your homework.
You've got to know where your people are, how many
you've registered. You've got to be able to say to a town
supervisor or legislator how many votes you have,
whom you can affect, and then you've got to organize
that vote so it can impact on that legislator.

"In upstate New York, we've got some state legislators who are so responsive to their black
constituents—and these are white legislators—because
of our being able to organize that black vote and show

that guy, 'Hey, man, you have forty thousand people voting in your Assembly district, and you won by fifteen hundred. Black people gave you two thousand votes. We own you, man.' He may not have known that. You need to have an organized system to take credit for that, because you know who takes credit for it now? The Republican town chairman or the Democratic town chairman. And these white guys go back and say to these white legislators, 'Oh, man, my niggers came out for you. You see what I did? I got my niggers out for you. They voted for you.' So what happens is that your vote keeps them in, but you don't even get the credit. So the legislator doesn't come and talk to you; he's not responsive; he doesn't even know you exist.

"You need to organize if for no other reason than so you can go in and say, 'We delivered those votes and now we want to talk to you.' And you may not have delivered *nothing*, but at least as an organized structure you can go in and say, 'We delivered those votes.' "

Sometimes, when people talk about separate power for their own group, it's scary. One can see a country being pulled apart, whites lined up against blacks, or one ethnic or religious group against another. But Eve's militancy is aimed at equality, not apartness. As we talked to him we felt we wanted the chance to work to get Eve elected. His vision of a place without poverty, without brutality, and where all people are

treated fairly grabbed us in a way that no one in public
life has for a long time. That he mixes this vision with
an understanding of practical politics is a double cause
for jubilation.

Eve's primary campaign for mayor of Buffalo is a
textbook on how to organize a minority to get one of its
own elected. He notes with relish that most of the
preprimary polls showed him losing. He won, he says,
because the kind of campaign he ran was not the kind
the white machine could counter easily. While his
opponents relied on mass media, neighborhood sound
trucks, and the clubhouse regulars to spread a fear of
Eve and what he would do if elected (Joseph Crangle,
the county chairman, called Eve a dangerous ultralib-
eral), Eve was mapping out a precise, grass-roots,
district-by-district battle plan. He learned it from Carl
Stokes, the former mayor of Cleveland.

"Carl taught me that effective politics is politics of
people. That you organize the masses. The historical
machine politician is always saying, 'I've got X number
of voters out there.' In the black community, it's
normally how many people you have on the payroll
and their families and friends. Carl said, 'Politics of
people means that you go at all of the people. You
identify every registered voter in the district, and you
set up a system on how to bring out every voter.' "

To this formula Eve added an idea of his own,
which was to announce early enough so as to give

people the incentive to register. He felt it was a lot more effective to run a voter registration drive among blacks if you could go to someone and say, "Hey, you've got to get registered so we can get our guy elected."

"I always felt that we could excite our community if we announced for an office and then ran the registration drive. In my campaign we registered people who had never voted before in their lives, but we did it after we announced and the campaign heightened, so people thought, 'This guy has a chance to win,' and then they had a reason to register."

Eve's campaign made use of Stokes's organizational lessons. In most campaigns, field operations are run from a central headquarters, usually with a large telephone bank, through which voters are contacted. All decisions are made from headquarters; all material is disseminated, and all voter canvassing is initiated, from there, even though several storefronts might operate around the city. (These are mostly for visibility in neighborhoods, a form of advertising rather than places that play an essential role in field operations.)

In Eve's campaign each election district became a self-contained headquarters, soliciting its own volunteers and organizing activities on a block-by-block basis within its boundaries. Overall precinct captains would be coordinators for ten of these E.D.s, and then each

E.D. would have one person responsible for its neighborhood operation. The E.D. leader reported to the captain, but each neighborhood basically made its own decisions about what material was needed, who would do which job, and so on. Everybody was found some job to do that would pull in another person.

"If a person was retired, didn't get out much, but liked to talk on the phone, he or she became our telephone system for that particular election district. We had another guy who drove cabs and loved to drive, but he didn't like to talk. He couldn't communicate. So he became our transportation."

The sharing of responsibility meant that each house in the district could be canvassed. Each block was somebody's responsibility. By systematic door-to-door canvassing, touching every family and every home, the campaign workers found many people who had never registered before. One was a ninety-two-year-old woman who didn't know that women *could* register and vote. She had no telephone or radio and she couldn't read. Eve's volunteers helped her fill out the proper registration form, showed her where to sign her X, and she voted for the first time in her life.

With such a broad-based campaign structure, Eve was able to ask volunteers to work no more than five hours a week. Because they didn't have to report to a centralized campaign headquarters, they could also work near their homes. Politicians would walk into

Eve's main headquarters and be appalled because there'd be only four or five people. "It was a real street campaign," insists Eve. "The thing that we know best *is* the streets, and that's where we have to be. Every Saturday morning, at nine A.M., our people canvassed, until twelve thirty, and then they would report back to their captains on what the responses were. That's the way you build accountability. They had to report to us every name of every individual whom they had talked to that day—who was not at home, whatever the case might be. When they'd report back, they might say, 'Man, we ran into this lady who said she won't vote for you under *no* circumstances!' and I'd say, 'What's her name?' Then I'd get on the phone and I'd sit for two or three hours and talk to these people personally. It's a matter of reaching out and saying, 'What is it? Why is it that you won't support me?' and nine times out of ten, unless they had a job at City Hall and that job was on the line, they would turn around and say, 'All right, man; you're all right.' They wanted that personal approach, that personal touch."

It was unusual for us to meet someone whose commitment to forcing change in the political system is so constant—someone who has been raising issues and fighting for certain principles all his life—and yet didn't make us feel uncomfortable for being less committed and less involved. Eve doesn't judge people; he doesn't feel the need to do it. In fact, he warns others about closing off anyone by making small judgments.

"Don't be mad if brothers can't come out front," he tells his audience, "if you know it's going to hurt them. Let me make that very clear: I had black guys who I helped get through college, law school, then to the point where they were working with the city. And when I ran for mayor some of them came to me and said, 'Man, they gave me your opponent's petition to circulate. It's killing me, I've got to circulate your opponent's petition. Mr. Eve, you've done too much for me. I can't do it. I'm going to quit my job.'

"I said, 'Hey, man, don't you quit that job. You've got a wife and a baby and you've got that house. Don't quit that job. You circulate that petition. Get those twenty-five signatures, but I want you to go back and talk to all them twenty-five people and make sure they vote for me, O.K.? And make sure you get your momma, your daddy, your brothers, your cousins, and anybody else who ain't got a city job to come over here and help me in this campaign.'

"A lot of times a lot of brothers get mad—'Hey, if you're not out front with me, you're an Uncle Tom; you're no good'—that rap, you know. Don't come down on the brothers and sisters. You give that brother or sister an opportunity to help. And don't cut him off! There's a lot of us who can be out front; and there's a lot of us who can be behind the scenes doing a very effective job. So give that brother and sister an opportunity to participate in the struggle with you. And if the bottom line to it is that he says, 'I can't do anything,' then you say, 'Well, brother, please don't hurt me. If you can't help me, then don't hurt me, and when you go into that voting machine, there ain't nobody there but you and God. Just go ahead and do what you have to do.' I have to repeat that: Give the brother and sister some role in the struggle. There is something that everyone can do."

Bill Bradley

☆

"The Great White Hope"

"He's going to be President some day." That's what people said when Bill Bradley was nineteen and beginning his freshman year at Princeton, where he would dominate the sport of college basketball. He has all the right credentials. He's white, upper middle class (his father was a prosperous banker from Crystal City, Missouri), Protestant, good-looking, hard-working, and self-disciplined. These qualities place him in the mainstream of American politicians and mean that he has a chance to reach the top. The odds are against anyone else in this book making it that far.

Bill Bradley is tall—and he looks even taller than he is. He has long arms, enormous hands, and a large head. He does not easily fit into a standard-size American car, which is where we interviewed him.

Bradley's ten years as a professional basketball player for the New York Knickerbockers put him in what is often regarded as the "blackest" of sports—black athletes have found a more open and successful route to the top in basketball than in any other sport. In fact, black players dominate the sport. Bradley entered this world already famous for his years on the Princeton squad and his gold medal in the Olympics, and he had to find his place within it. Because he had signed with the Knicks for a then astronomical sum of money, he was given the nickname "Dollar Bill." He was also called, although not as openly in the press, "The Great White Hope." It was assumed that Bradley had planned his future and was using basketball to make a lot of money and, more important, gain a national reputation that would enable him to enter politics at a high level. Bradley feels this assumption about him was a bum rap.

"What can I tell you?" he says. "Because I was the Great White Hope, because I liked to read books, which was strange because I was an athlete; because I, like millions of other people said, 'Yeah, politics interests me'—suddenly I was supposed to be planning this career, which is just not the way things happen in life."

Still in 1965, when Bradley was graduating from Princeton, writer John McPhee did a profile of the college star and said, "I have asked all sorts of people who know Bradley, or know about him, what they think he will be doing when he is forty. A really startling number of them, including teachers, coaches, college boys, and even journalists, give the same

answer: 'He will be the governor of Missouri.'"*
Thirteen years later, Bradley has achieved a seat in the
U.S. Senate from New Jersey at the age of thirty-five.
It is not a great departure from the prediction.

For a while, Bradley thought his natural political
base would be his home state, Missouri. In the last
years of his career with the Knicks, it was rumored he
was checking out the situation there—taking polls and
seeking support from politicians—with an eye toward
running for state office as secretary of state. He decided
to stay in the East, however, and found a not unwelcome environment in New Jersey, where Knick
fans are numerous and politicians do not last as long in
office as they do in more stable political climates.
Bradley moved to the suburban community of Den-
ville in 1972 and began campaigning for selected
Democratic candidates and tickets.

Given the way things have turned out for him, it's
still a fact that Bradley did not really plan it all. A lot of
it "just happened."

"Whoever heard of springing into politics from
professional basketball? Five years ago, if you would
have said, 'Could somebody leave professional basketball and win a U.S. Senate seat?' you would have said
no. But that does nothing more than point out the
error of categories. I thought I would only be a

*John McPhee, *A Sense of Where You Are* (New York: Bantam, 1965), p. 25.

professional basketball player for four years. I thought it would end after four years; and I was wrong, because I came to be able to admit to myself that I loved what I was doing. And I saw no reason why I had to take other people's advice, like 'If you want to do X or Y, you'd better stop playing,' and, 'If you want to be in politics, you have to do X, Y, and Z to prepare yourself.' Five or six kids have said to me, 'I want to be in politics; what should I do?' And I tell them, 'Go out and live life until you're thirty.' People who get in really early lose those years of experimentation—personal experimentation. I think that ultimately they're not as good at what they're doing, because their life isn't broadened."

Bradley was drafted by the Knicks immediately after he graduated from Princeton, where he was named All-American. The New York team assumed he would start playing right away. Instead, he chose to accept a Rhodes Scholar fellowship to Oxford University in England, where he spent the next two years forgetting about basketball altogether. He had no plans to return to the sport when his fellowship ended.

"I became freer when I went to England," he recalls. "There's a real parallel with physicality, because when I was in college, I was very superprotective of my body." As he says this, he pats himself on the chest sheepishly. It is the first and only time in our interview that he seems to be making fun of himself. "And one of the real liberating forces at Oxford was that I didn't care if I got hurt, so I did what I thought were incredibly dangerous things: raced cars, played rugby once or twice until I really didn't like it. I think that feeling also led to a belief that you had to, you know, probe life."

In his book, *Life on the Run*, Bradley explores this feeling further. "Eating five meals a day, I even gained thirty pounds. I questioned my religious faith and sought workable moral values instead of simply rules. I became more playful and rebellious, responding to events in a way that discipline and obligation had outlawed before. I stopped taking myself so seriously, recognizing that life is as much a good laugh as a stirring sermon.

"Towards the end of my second year, after not touching a basketball for nine months, I went to the Oxford gym, simply for some long overdue exercise. There I shot alone, just the ball, the basket, and my imagination. As I heard the swish and felt my body loosening to familiar movements, the jumper, the hook, the reverse pivot, I could hear the crowd though I was alone on the floor. . . . I realized that I missed the game. . . . I knew that never to play again, never to play against the best, the pros, would be to deny an aspect of my personality perhaps more fundamental than any other. Three weeks later I signed a contract with the New York Knicks."*

Bradley's style of play during his ten years with the Knicks can best be described as "team ball." The game has always had its hotshots, dazzling playmakers, and one-on-one masters. Bradley was capable of making the astounding play, but he usually chose not to. He was not an innovator. His selfless emphasis on working as part of a team, giving up the personal game and looking for the open man, won him much respect but also some criticism. Butch van Breda Kolff, his coach at Princeton, often had to remind Bradley that *he* was an open man too, and should shoot the ball himself instead of always trying to pass it off. He also had to deal with Bradley's superserious approach to the game, and once said of his star player, "Basketball is a game. It is not an ordeal. I think Bradley's happiest whenever he can deny himself pleasure." After Bradley's years in England, the seriousness lessened, but his style of play remained the same.

Part of the reason why Bradley played team ball was that he always felt he was not a natural athlete. His teammates used to joke that he was the only player in the league with the body of an eighty-year-old-man, that when Bradley jumped for a shot, you could fit no

*Bill Bradley, *Life on the Run* (New York: Quadrangle, 1976), pp. 35–36.

more than one daily *New York Times* between his feet and the floor. Bradley has said that even when he was in peak condition, he never could do what other, more naturally gifted athletes could. He couldn't lift a barbell, he said, without a winch; and "standing legs straight, I can't touch the floor with anything but my feet." Still, Bradley is an uncommonly well-coordinated and physically talented athlete, and an alleged lack of physical gifts is not only untrue but an insufficient explanation of why he played the way he did.

Bradley actually defines basketball as a team game. He says that every minute of the game reflects collective team efforts and decisions. He enjoyed that aspect of the game enormously, but he says it differs from what he has seen so far of politics.

"I haven't yet experienced that same sense of narrow community that exists in sports. Maybe that sense is there in the Senate, maybe it's among a group of senators, maybe it'll be there among my staff; but there's an absence of clearly defined and accepted and universal collective responsibility, which is built into the structure of sports. I mean, if I miss a shot at the end of the game, I missed it—that's right—but you fit it into the context. Why was I the one who ended up taking the shot? Because everybody had decided that I was the shooter. That was my role. It was, in a way, an indirect but collective decision. I didn't lose the game;

the team lost the game, because the game was lost in the first quarter, when so-and-so made three errors, as much as it was lost in the last shot.

"In politics you find a lot of people who say, 'We think you should do this,' but when you do it and it turns out to be wrong, they don't say, 'Well, that was *our* mistake.' I think that's not the fault of any of the people, but it's a fact of their job. It is you who will make the decision and will make the judgment. And in that sense it is a more solitary life, in the most personal sense."

In our interview with Bradley, we were a little reluctant to jump into the sports-politics connection. It seemed so obvious to draw parallels between the two fields that we almost went out of our way to avoid mentioning his past career. To our surprise, however, Bradley kept bringing it up, seeing all sorts of similarities or lessons in the two activities.

"I think the competitiveness of the campaign is very similar—not to a game but to a whole season. You're subject to the same highs and lows based upon performances. Some days you think you're terrible. Other days you think you're the best. And somewhere in between is the truth. And you have to keep that perspective or you will be subject to personality changes that are destructive. I dealt with that as an athlete in the professional ranks, and I was thus able to transfer it easily to these situations. I had not accomplished that in sports at college. When we lost, I was shot for a day or two; when we won, I was very pleased. But only when I was a professional playing four times a week did I realize that if you lost all that emotional energy when each game was over, instead of preparing for the next battle, there was no way you could survive. I had to learn not to carry the emotional baggage of success or defeat with me."

Bradley is a tough competitor; he was known in sports for never letting up, no matter how far the team was ahead or behind. In his Senate race in 1978 against Jeffrey Bell, Bradley was acknowledged from the start to be way ahead. Every poll showed him ahead during the entire campaign. Bell was a young new-comer to politics who had defeated the long-time Republican incumbent, Senator Clifford Case, in the primary. Bell was perceived as being from the right wing of the Republican party—his campaign focused almost exclusively on a call for a massive federal tax cut—and in a not uncommon feat, he was able to knock off the more moderate and much older Case. But when it came to the general election, Bell's views seemed far from the center, whereas Bradley's, called "just left of center," lay closer to most voters' senti-ments. Bradley was much better known, too, and he had stayed out of past political battles in the state and thus had few enemies among New Jersey politicians. Also to most voters he seemed a "decent guy"—not flashy, not overly articulate or too fast on his feet, just someone a voter could identify with. He was way ahead of Bell from the start of the campaign, and no one thought for a moment that he wouldn't win the election.

But you couldn't tell that by watching Bradley. He campaigned as if he were the underdog moving within an inch or two of catching a front-runner. His workers were heard to complain that he was overdoing it, overscheduling himself and them, overworrying, over-speaking, overblanketing the press with his releases. "It's in the bag," they'd say. "Why is he being so compulsive about it?" As proof of his compulsion, they'd cite the fact that Bradley agreed at the start to debate Bell as often as possible. He scheduled twenty-one debates with Bell over a two-month period, thus breaking every known political rule of campaigning. Traditionally the front-runner, especially if he is already well known, will not agree to debate an opponent who is (1) not as well known; (2) more articulate in public speaking; and (3) has no way except a debate to get his views and personality across. But Bradley looked at it differently.

"One of the reasons for scheduling twenty-one debates," he explained, "was because I felt I was always better as an athlete if I'd gotten very familiar with the terrain—knew the opponents—because the unknown was always the worst opponent. So I was willing to schedule twenty-one debates, because by the time the debates would count, in the last two or three weeks of the campaign, I'd know the other guy's moves.

"Everyone said, 'You're crazy. You're ahead. Why do you want to debate the man twenty-one times?' But when the debates counted, I wanted to know my opponent. There were other reasons, too. I legitimately felt that it was important in this campaign for the people of New Jersey to know our opposing positions. . . . That's where self-confidence comes in, and also an assessment of what Bell's views were. I knew that I was not the greatest speaker, but that didn't bother me. I felt very strongly that it would not come down to how my views were presented but what my views were. And the more people who knew them, I felt, the better off I was."

Though he became more adept by the end of the campaign, Bradley's speaking style would win no prizes. In a flat tone and almost expressionless face, he could go on for a half hour reciting—(sometimes it seemed as if he'd actually memorized) his speech. As he did it more, though, he loosened up and spoke better. But he still recalls some of the all-time lows in his campaign, which more than once had to do with a "disastrous speech."

"I remember in the campaign I spoke—I addressed—the state American Legion Convention. I had gotten up at a quarter of five in the morning to get

there—it was way down at the Jersey shore—and first
of all, the sergeant-at-arms, or the security officer for
the convention, told me I couldn't wear my campaign
button because it was a nonpolitical event. So I took
my button off, and when I walked into the convention,
very few people said hello. Then I walked to the front
of the room and climbed the steps to the podium and
tripped. Then I reached for a glass of water on the table
and knocked it off into the front row. Then I got up to
give my speech, and I realized two paragraphs into it
that it was the wrong speech. I don't mean that I had
taken a copy of another speech that I hadn't meant to
give, but that the subject I had chosen for this event
was the wrong subject. It didn't really matter anyway,
because no one was listening to me. Ten minutes into
the speech, the chairman came up to the podium
where I was standing and said, 'Will you please give
the speaker some attention?' Then I concluded the
speech and left. I was feeling pretty low, thinking
maybe it had been a disastrous moment. Now it
sounds humorous, but at the time it wasn't so
humorous.

"You tell yourself two things after an event like that.
First, that no one event will determine the campaign;
and the other, that you've got to have a sense of
humor. I always found in the campaign that except for
the most extreme moments of tension, what revived
me was contact with people. We would always

schedule, after a particularly tense meeting, a people event, where I would go out and shake hands, because those events always reminded me of several things. First of all, nobody knew what had just happened except you and maybe four or five other people; and second, the problems that you sometimes focus on in a campaign are not the real things that bother people."

A "people event" to most politicians means pressing flesh. There's a "high" to be gotten from going out, smiling, and shaking a thousand hands in one hour. Some politicians start out their careers by recoiling from this kind of transitory touching, but they soon learn to live with it. Most people in politics—and this is true of women as well as men—seem to love it. People are genuinely nice to them, they say. This is easy to believe. How many people would be rude to a well-dressed, smiling person standing with hand extended, introducing himself but letting you know that he won't take but a few seconds of your time. Candidates tell you they feel "replenished" after such contact. To people in the nonpolitical world, listening to a politician explain how he's making "real people connections" this way, or how he's really getting to "know people" through this process, suspends belief. It is just as hard to believe Bill Bradley when he talks about the "insights" he gets from such events: "insights into the personalities of human beings, sometimes expressed in anger, sometimes in joy, indifference, the whole thing; it's that human dimension that always puts the whole thing into perspective."

Though he can sound ingenuous about campaigning, Bradley also has a shrewd understanding of the role personality plays in politics. At these times, he stops sounding like any old politician. He is good at assessing people and their motivations, and is sensitive to the personal interactions of politics. He says that the greatest surprise to him was to see how important a role personality does play in politics. When he was a kid, he says, he thought politics was basically a matter of speeches and taking worthwhile positions.

"I think it's fascinating, because you really see some aberrations in this business. Not aberrations in the sense of being sick, but aberrations in the sense of what stress does to a personality. Like a mayor who reminisces about his childhood in order to make a point about a particular bill or a particular need; or a political party official who is unnecessarily interested in winning a particularly meaningless battle, and therefore he puts all of his chits in that battle. When you offer no resistance, he doesn't know how to react. His big reference point is that this should be a battle and that superior power should prevail. And frequently, that's the way it's conducted out there. So when you redefine the game on the basis of personality evaluation or sensitivity, they don't know what to do a lot of the time.

"There are some rules in politics—that are always broken"—he pauses again and laughs—"if the moment is appropriate. There's a certain level of civility that people like to believe about politics. At political dinners, the skilled political person always acknowledges in an ingratiating and perhaps mocking way, every dignitary at the head table. I fooled around occasionally, and intentionally have not done it, just to see what the reaction would be. And the reaction among some of the political figures was reminiscent of the temper tantrums of a five-year-old. They took it as a grave insult. But that's how I learned, in a way, where you experiment and deal with personalities. When a person reacts that way it tells you something about that person."

Bradley won the election easily. He had taken forthright stands: he did not equivocate on his support for the right to abortion, on greater aid to the cities, and on increased dollars to human services. Like many "new" politicians, he is very interested in solar energy and other aspects of the fuel question. In the Senate he plans to make that topic and finance his two chief concerns.

"I want to be on Finance and Energy, those committees; I want to work on alternate sources of energy, and I'd like to be on the Finance Committee to go to work on what I call the nitty-gritty issues—taxes, welfare reform, unemployment compensation—all the issues that really very few people in this country understand. I'd like to be able to think through some positions that would benefit New Jersey. At the same time, I'd like to be able to speak out on national questions, what I see as the increasing polarities in the country, and the long-run problems that come from a divided society. . . . Trying to get through to people that it's in the national interest to husband and target those ever-scarcer resources, instead of spreading government money all over."

Bradley gives as an example the Elementary and Secondary School Education Act, whose purpose was to spend money on programs for disadvantaged children. The quid pro quo for passage of the act, however, diluted the aid so that less money went to inner cities and more to small, rural communities. Bradley says, "That's where the real need *isn't*. I want a chance to speak out on such resource allocation issues.

"I think you have to choose the issues on which you can exert your leadership. I don't think you can exert leadership on every issue. You lose your credibility."

Bradley's move to Washington will mean a temporary separation from his wife and infant daughter. His wife, Dr. Ernestine Schlant, plans to remain in New Jersey until the end of her semester at Montclair State College, where she is a professor of German literature. They will alternate on weekends until then, each commuting one weekend in order to see the other. Next year, Dr. Schlant will take a year of absence from school and move to Washington, where part of her time will be spent on research for a new book (she has authored five books). When we had asked Bradley what he considered the worst thing about politics, he first gave the answer, "What it does to your family life," but right away he said, "No that's not it" and went on to discuss the role of personality in politics. At this point it looks as if the independence of both Bradley and Dr. Schlant means they'll have an easier time than most in coping with the strains that politics often put on a marriage.

Bradley has been accused of taking himself too seriously. His constant introspection has given him strict standards for himself and others, but it has also given him a sense of life's absurdity and the need to not always take himself too seriously. In his book he refers to a favorite dream: It's the last shot of the game. He is standing at the free-throw line, having been fouled with only eight seconds left to play. The other team is ahead by one point. He needs to make the shot to tie it up. Bradley, who went through Princeton with the highest free-throw percentage of any college player, who in the pros rarely missed a foul shot, gets into position, raises the ball high over his head, and throws it twenty feet over the backboard. "And I laugh, and laugh, and laugh, and laugh."

We asked him if he ever felt like doing something totally absurd like that in politics.

"Sure, yeah," he says, with a spontaneous smile as if right away he thought of something he isn't going to tell. "Did I ever do it in the campaign? No, I don't think I ever did it in the campaign." He pauses, reconsidering. "Well, that urge," he says, pausing again, "well, I say I didn't do it in the campaign, but sometimes, when the tension is great, or the question so absurd, you pick a person and you unload on one person out there, and then you move on. Dump a little of the baggage that you've accumulated. The key thing is not to do it on staff, because if you do it on staff, life becomes unpleasant. But let's say you run into a guy at a cocktail party who is suddenly blistering you about politicians and you and life. Obviously, he's somebody who's unhappy with himself, but he's decided that *you're* the problem. So you unload on him. You tell him a few things. You can always see their faces when it happens, 'cause it's so out of character. A politician is supposed to say only nice things, and ingratiate himself. And if you tell the guy that he's a real jerk, his mouth drops. None of them ever say, 'Well, I'll vote against you for that,' which is your fear, which is why some people don't do it."

Bradley's sense of the absurd, of perhaps in the future being willing to take risks greater than insulting one rude voter at a party (which most politicians would

not dare to do), may make him more than a Great
White Hope. For someone who has just run his first
campaign and has been elected to his first office—and
at a level where he did not have to take on the power
structure and its tendency to force conformity—it's too
early to tell.

Tom Hayden

☆

"You Can't Personally Start a Movement, No Matter How Much You Want It"

"Is that Tom Hayden?" a young woman asks us as a short, dark-haired man in a doubleknit suit climbs the stairs toward the huge pillars of Shriver Hall at Johns Hopkins University in Baltimore. The woman, dressed conservatively herself, is very nervous.

She has every right to be. She is the student co-coordinator for a lecture series entitled "Retrospective on the Sixties: From Camelot to Chaos," and this afternoon Tom Hayden is the featured speaker. The lecture is scheduled for four o'clock. Hayden had promised to be there by three, and it's now ten minutes to four. The audience has begun to pile into the auditorium, and soon it is filled to capacity with over five hundred people.

We are in as bad shape as the young woman. Hayden's schedule is so tight on his visit East that the only time he could fit in our interview was for the hour before his lecture. We agreed to go to Baltimore to meet him but must be in South Carolina the next morning for another interview. For an organizer during the Sixties, and one of our peer group, Hayden is going to have a lot of explaining to do. It's supposed to be the old pols who overschedule, arrive late, and keep you waiting.

We tell the young woman that the man in the doubleknit suit is not Tom Hayden. "I don't know what he looks like," she confides. Then she and we play the game of trying to remain calm while each of us secretly schemes how to get to Hayden before the other.

At about five minutes after four, a short, harassed-looking man wearing a raincoat, tan pants, and sports jacket and tie runs purposefully up the stairs. He says to the first person he sees, "I'm awfully sorry. We've been stuck in traffic. It's terrible." He does not explain whether the traffic or his lateness is terrible.

The student reception committee wins the first round. They, after all, have five hundred people waiting and have paid $1500 for Hayden that day. There are only two of us. Hayden comes up to us and shakes our hands, muttering more apologies.

"Can we get an interview afterward?" we ask.

Before he can answer, the student committee tries, almost forcibly, to shove him down the stairs to the stage anteroom.

"I'll try to give you some time," he calls back to us,

"but ask a lot of questions during the lecture and I'll just keep calling on you."

This is going to be our first interview conducted in front of five hundred people. Of the different politicians we approached for this book, Hayden was far and away the hardest to pin down. It wasn't difficult to get him to say yes to the interview, but from then on it was like trying to catch a greased pig. We had been given the go-ahead for Baltimore by his staff only the night before, with assurances of at least an hour alone with him. Now even that looked chancy.

Resigned, we walk into the auditorium. Seated behind us are two reporters from the school paper. One says to the other, "Who is he, anyhow?"

"He was married to Jane Fonda. I read that in *People* magazine."

"Is he still married to her?"

"I don't know."

Hayden is thirty-eight. These students must be about nineteen. That would mean they were four or five years old at the time Hayden became famous for his political activities. In the Sixties, you wouldn't have had to ask, "Who is he?" Hayden was the most charismatic leader to emerge from the student revolutionary movement.

"Blessed with an instinct for being in the right place at the right time" is how Kirkpatrick Sale described him. In 1960 Hayden was a student at the University

of Michigan, editor of the school newspaper. He had
spent the previous summer at Berkeley in California,
"soaking up," as he puts it, the beginnings of the
student movement and the politics of the left. "I got
radicalized," Hayden says. "*No one* is born that way."
He came back to Michigan and co-founded a student
party. Within a short time he had joined the Students
for a Democratic Society (SDS), not yet a real
organization but simply a small group of people, most
of them at Michigan or in New York, who owned a
mimeograph machine. In the fall of 1961, Hayden,
who had by now graduated from college, became
SDS's field secretary in the South. He was to work with
the Student Nonviolent Coordinating Committee
(SNCC) on its voter registration drive and report on the
civil rights movement blossoming there. He spent his
twenty-second birthday in a jail cell in Albany,
Georgia. His reports, which were mimeographed and
sent by the national SDS office to colleges around the
country, detailed the brutality of working in the
South—the beatings, killings, and incarcerations of
students, most of them black, who were organizing
black voters. Hayden saw them as "in more danger
than nearly any student in this American generation
has faced."

What Hayden took from the experience was a
growing sense that young people could make a
difference, that they could be organized into a move-

ment for change that went beyond civil rights issues. "The civil rights movement was the most important issue at the time in terms of mobilizing people," he said, "but it didn't speak to the total needs of students, who were just then becoming socially conscious."*

Hayden saw that it was possible to link small movements into a larger one. His analysis of society stretches wide enough to include the economic, social, and political aspects. He sees the foreign affairs symptoms of what is wrong with us as well as the domestic ones, the historic as well as the current perspective. The first draft of the Port Huron Statement for SDS, which became *the* document of the student movement, was a searing indictment of American society. It began, "We are people of this generation, bred in at least moderate comfort, housed now in universities, looking uncomfortably to the world we inherit." It then went on to dissect America's ills and covered everything from the bomb to big labor unions, from big business to unresponsive political parties, from racial discrimination to military-industrial power. It did more. It offered a vision of what could be: a sense of community, a sense of democracy that was not just limited to a ritual in a voting booth, but was a larger "participatory democracy." Those words became the hallmark of the New Left.

Hayden spent months drafting the Port Huron

*From an unpublished interview with Hayden by George R. Vickers, Venice, California, August 23, 1971.

Statement, reading everything he could get his hands on that might be pertinent to social upheaval: works by C. Wright Mills, Harold Taylor, Albert Camus, Eric Fromm, David Riesman, Michael Harrington, Iris Murdock, and Norman O. Brown. Ask anyone who knows Hayden—even those who fought with him during movement days or since—and they will say, "Hayden is smart, very smart."

College editor of the prestigious Michigan *Daily*, chief theoretician of the New Left, drafter of the Port Huron Statement. Those are Hayden's intellectual credits. But Hayden wanted to be more than that. At the point when SDS was coming into its own as a national organization (by 1963 it had nine hundred dues-paying members and over twenty college chapters), Hayden went off to organize the poor in Newark, New Jersey. He wrote at the time, "We are trying to organize, first around the feeling of being poor and powerless, rather than being black. . . . We are also trying to organize so that poor people develop a consciousness of themselves as worthwhile human beings. Flashy demonstrations don't interest us that much. By insisting the poor can make decisions, we are striking at all of the society's pretense, respectability, and hierarchy."* Hayden left the leadership of SDS to others and spent three years in Newark.

*From Jack Newfield, *A Prophetic Minority* (New York: Signet, 1966), p. 105.

All his adult life, Hayden has been identified as a "leader"; even in Newark, the press tried to point to him as chief of the operation. But Hayden has an ambivalence about personal leadership and backs away from it as often as he makes use of it. In Newark he would say he was not a leader but an organizer. "The organizer must spend hours and hours listening to people . . . rejecting their tendency to depend on him for solutions. . . . Only in this way can a movement be built which the Establishment can neither buy off nor manage."*

It's ironic that the system Hayden has opposed is continually identifying him as a leader. After the disruption and violence at the 1968 Democratic National Convention in Chicago, when it was decided by those in power that someone would have to be blamed for what happened, Tom Hayden was a natural selection as one of the few to take the blame. He and six others were convicted of conspiracy to cross state lines and instigate a riot. At the trial Hayden said, "We were invented. We were chosen by the Government to serve as scapegoats for all that they wanted to prevent happening in the 1970's." His conviction was later overturned.

At that trial, Judge Julius J. Hoffman said to him,

*From Kirpatrick Sale, SDS (New York: Random House, Vintage Books, 1974), p. 133.

"You know, a fellow as smart as you could go an awfully long way within the system." Today, Hayden says sardonically, "So I decided to take his advice." In 1976 he ran for the U.S. Senate in California's Democratic primary, pulling 37 percent of the vote with his theme that "the radicalism of the Sixties is the common sense of the Seventies."

The press delights in pointing to Hayden's marriage to movie star Jane Fonda and his entry into two-party politics. It seems to be saying, "See, now you realize the system *can* work, and the radical excess of your youth wasn't necessary, was probably even harmful."

Hayden thinks there is a despicable attempt going on to rewrite the history of the Sixties and pretend that America as a nation agreed all along on what was wrong and what to do about it. "I believe it is possible," he says, "for a movement to make great achievements and then lose a lot of them to those who write the history later. I happen to believe that the Sixties was *the* most important single decade of the twentieth century, and I believe that the full impact of the Sixties will not be felt until the Eighties or Nineties.

"It's not true that liberals, conservatives, and radicals all agree now that women should have equal rights. It is not true that we all agree that the cold war was a bad thing. There is now an attempt on the part of many people who were the most ferocious proponents of segregation, and sexism, and war, to make it seem that they were against those things all along.

"In the course of history, I hope people will see that the firebombing of Vietnam was a truly radical excess, and that those students who demonstrated in the streets against it were doing what their parents ought to have been doing but did not do."

Hayden comes from a middle-class family who lived in a suburb outside Detroit. He was reared a Catholic and went to parochial schools, although his parents later divorced. He went to college on a tennis scholarship, and majored in English, joining the staff of the school newspaper. Up to that point, he says, the influences on his life were not political but cultural, and that he was greatly affected by the Beat Generation: James Dean movies, J. D. Salinger's *Catcher in the Rye*, the novels of Jack Kerouac, and the poems of Allen Ginsberg and Lawrence Ferlinghetti. In the late 1950's, Hayden hitchhiked to selected spots around the country— Greenwich Village, New Orleans's French Quarter, and San Francisco.

"My high school involvement in politics had always been with the negative approach. This was before there was politics. There was *Mad* magazine. *Mad* magazine was considered very rebellious. We had the first underground paper that we called the *Daily Smirker*; we thought it was a great play on the *Daily Worker* [the communist newspaper], and we just generally caused problems. It wouldn't have been considered politics then."

The message of *Mad* magazine and the Beats was that you looked around at what was wrong and either laughed at it (*Mad*'s motto was "What, me worry?") or just withdrew entirely.

But in the spring of 1960 Hayden saw that the sit-ins and demonstrations by black students in the South were evidence that direct action could be taken and could have an impact. He began to see that students could come out of isolation; and with that he began to envision a national student movement.

The student movement that came into existence— SDS was its embodiment—went beyond Hayden's earliest dreams. Throughout the Sixties the movement was to change the focus of its actions many times— from civil rights in the South to urban ghetto organization, from anti-Vietnam activities to the violent bomb-throwing of the Weathermen, SDS's final form. Hayden was never far from the action. He might not have been there at the beginning of each new attack-front, but as soon as he began to see its possibilities, he was ready to move on it. Hayden also fought to keep SDS vague and nonideological so that anyone who wanted to work for social change could feel part of its community.

"To get a mass following," he says, "you have to

have a cause that's very simple, very concrete, and very just. Like 'End the war in Vietnam.' But in order to get leadership, to get the people who will organize, their dedication has to be for something much more far-reaching than simply to end the war; because they're out there sacrificing their comfort, sacrificing their income, their status, possibly their lives, certainly their reputations and their time. It's exhausting work. It's demanding work. And in order to make that kind of sacrifice, one has to have very, very wild dreams—a far-reaching vision, far ahead of what the mass members of an organization will have. Then they come to a point where they end the war, but by then that doesn't satisfy them. They have become so radicalized. They are frustrated at the moment of winning.

"That's a problem I think that organizers always have to cope with. But to me the optimistic lesson is that movements succeed. They are then transformed; people go back to work; everything levels off. But that doesn't mean the movement is dead. In the case of the 1960's, the organizers, the leaders, the people who did the hard work, were not so frustrated or handicapped, or ruined by the experience, that they see no further life ahead. That's a myth that has to be blown away, that the movement leaders and the activists have all become bankers, insurance salesmen, or peddlers of some weird biblical concepts. The press loves the fact

that I married a movie star. But don't let appearances
fool you, because what has really happened is that the
Sixties are infiltrating the Seventies, the people who
were in the streets are now becoming more influen-
tial."

As Tom Hayden talks about what he is doing in the
Seventies, particularly his running for Senate, we
listen warily. We watch him for slips, for signs of a
sellout or a drastic turnaround in conviction. Yet, as
we look through everything he's written or said in the
past ten years—during his Senate campaign as well as
before or since—there is nothing to indicate a cave-in.
His criticisms, his attacks on the social, economic, and
political systems, and his outrage are all still there in
unequivocal language—perhaps rambling and too
long, but that was always true of his writing. The only
things that seem to have changed about Hayden are his
wealth and, perhaps, his access to traditional power.
His convictions, instincts, even his quirks (the policy
papers for his Senate campaign, written by him, ran on
for pages, sometimes making the same points twelve
different ways), remain the same. And he is still in the
organizing business.

Hayden is now chairperson of another organization
he has founded, the California Campaign for Economic Democracy. And, true to form, Hayden's
organization can't seem to decide on its name or how
large an assault it will make. Some of the group's

letterhead says, "California Campaign for Economic Democracy"; other stationery reads, "The Campaign for Economic Democracy." One senses another vision of another large movement dancing in Hayden's head.

CED looks formless and hard to define (exactly the complaints that were made about SDS). CED is active in promoting publicly controlled solar energy for the state, and Hayden has been appointed by Governor Jerry Brown to be California's solar energy "ambassador" to Washington. But the organization has other aims—it lobbies for low-income housing, welfare rights, and the opening up of private corporations to public influence and management.

CED runs a camp in remote hills high above Santa Barbara, California, called the Laurel Springs Children's Camp. Here, children of varied racial and economic backgrounds live in an experimental working community. Hayden, Fonda, and others in their group call Laurel Springs "The Land." Hayden is said to have referred to it as "Our Palestine." He and Fonda see it as a place where the movement still lives; a place where children can learn that change is possible if people commit themselves to working together for it.

The Campaign for Economic Democracy also puts up candidates for a wide range of offices in California, from local boards of education to mayors of large cities. It trains members in the political arts of canvassing, voter registration, precinct captaining, and other grass-roots organizing skills. In almost all cases, CED candidates run in Democratic primaries.

Hayden explains, "Most of the voters we want to reach—the poor, the minorities, the senior citizens, the consumers, the workers—are registered Democrats, if they're registered at all. To ask them to switch registration and join a new party they haven't heard of is unrealistic and unpractical. It only leads to the Republicans winning. So what we did was to form our own organization that's like a political party, but we compete with the traditional Democrats in their conventions and in their primaries. With some Democrats we have very good relations because they share our philosophy; with other Democrats we have off-and-on relations—sometimes we agree and sometimes we don't; and with other Democrats, we're like two opposing camps."

It's clear that Hayden, too, will run again. We ask him about his political future, having heard rumors of another Senate try or a possible run for mayor of Los Angeles. He's coy about answering, but says it's certain he'll run for something. "It would be irresponsible for me not to." We want to laugh at that remark. We have yet to hear a politician (radical or otherwise) who doesn't have a "good reason" for running, based on "others" wanting him or her to do it. We look to see if he's grinning as he delivers his rationale, but he is not.

"It would be wrong for me to run for office once,

with everybody who supported me, except me, thinking I was going to lose, and then turn around and say,
'Ha, I did it for nothing. I just feel like being a
journalist now,' or something like that. I have an
obligation to run again or otherwise I should not have
run in the first place. What I run for, or when, is
totally up in the air. It could be twelve years from now
frankly. It could be four years from now. It has to be
decided by a whole organization, by many people
beyond myself. I could decide the first time, but I am
no longer alone in this. And what I do or what happens
to me will affect other people very, very much. If I ran,
for example, and got 1.3 million votes, which would
be more votes than I got last time, I would then be
described as having failed, even though I did better
than the last time. I can't afford to go off and run and
get a lot of votes and have it described as a defeat,
because then the defeat would be for all these other
people in our organization. It would be very demoral-
izing."

Meanwhile, Hayden is active in other campaigns,
apparently hoping to see his organization play a large
role in the 1980 presidential primaries. He explains
that the CED cannot yet "go national," but will work
to train and energize other groups in states that have
primaries in 1980.

After his speech, we and about fifty other people
follow Hayden upstairs to a reception. Hayden had

planned to leave right after the speech (people are waiting for him in a Washington restaurant he says), but because of his lateness in arriving, he has promised to stay for a while. In the reception room, chocolate chip cookies and punch are grabbed, and a tight circle of questioners forms around him. We are in the circle's center trying to continue our questions. One young man keeps loudly interrupting, mostly asking about various rock groups and the role of rock music in politics. It soon becomes clear that he has been promised an interview too—he shoves his recorder just under Hayden's beltline. As we are finally getting in some questions of our own, the Student Reception Committee tugs Hayden and says, "That'll be all, we have to go to dinner now." We are not invited, but Hayden motions us to follow, and we spend the next fifteen minutes walking over the cold, rocky John Hopkins campus dragging our luggage, cameras, and other equipment, always trying to keep our recorder no more than a foot away from what he says.

"What was the difference between the organizing you did in the Sixties and your own campaign for Senate?" we want to know.

"The biggest difference between the organizing I did then and running for Senate is that *I* ran for the Senate; meaning that when you run for office, you get an awful lot of personality. The issue is you. You can say the issue is solar energy, but really what people are trying to analyze is you. And that's a difference that can't be erased.

"Then there's this idea that youth is permanent, that youth is perpetual. And there is this additional idea that there could be two economics—one for "them" and one for us. And that somehow we could get by. Very few people can do that. Until I married my wife, I had no money, no medical insurance; I had a thirteen-year-old Volkswagen, I had a hundred-dollar-a-month two-room apartment. That's fine if that's you. But most people want to hook up, want to live with somebody. Then a certain percentage want to have kids. If you have kids, you have to be able to pay for a doctor. It's totally irresponsible to say, 'I want to have a kid and to hell with the kid if he ever gets sick.' You can't do that. The test would be that if a real, radical crisis occurred again, would the activists of the Sixties sit it out or would they be in there? I think they'd be in there. You can't personally start a movement, no matter how much you want it. Someone will start a new one, but they won't plan it."

Polly Baca-Barragan

———————— ☆ ————————

"I Never Thought I'd Ever Meet a Politician, Let Alone Be One"

"You should interview Polly Baca-Barragan out in Colorado. She's a powerhouse," said Betsy Wright, executive director of the National Women's Education Fund, when we asked for suggestions for our book. "She's Chicano, young, strong on all the right issues, and she's gotten pretty far. She's in the State House of Representatives out there. She's running for state senator now and has been able to talk her possible opponents out of running against her. So it looks like she'll be in."

It seemed too good to be true. A woman politician already in office on her way up who is outspoken on issues like women's rights, abortion, migrant workers' conditions, and justice. We did a little research and found that while a freshman representative from Thornton, Colorado, she sponsored or co-sponsored 156 pieces of legislation that became law. This is an unheard of accomplishment for a newcomer in state government. She had also been elected chairman of the Democratic Caucus, a job requiring the greatest political savvy. We decided we had to fly out to Colorado to see her. She was to be our first interview.

Thornton is very near the Denver airport. The houses are neat little prefabricated ranchhouses and modern garden-apartment complexes called town-houses. We parked under her carport, "right next to my blue Pinto," as she had told us.

She seemed a little shy when she greeted us at the door. A small woman in her thirties, dressed in casual but conservative slacks, she looked as if she were settling in for a comfortable evening at home.

"Would you like something to drink?" she offers. "Perhaps a soda?" We go into her living room and sit down. The television is on upstairs, quite loudly. "It's the Miss Universe contest," she tells us. "My daughter is watching it." This is not quite the TV fare we'd expect from a feminist politician, and we're worried that our tape recorder will not pick up what we say over the noise. Still, we begin our explanation of why we have come to see her.

"This will be a book about people like yourself, who are working for change," we explain. "We wanted you because you represent a constituency that has been either underrepresented or not represented at all before." Polly Baca-Barragan begins to laugh, and we join in, though we don't know exactly why.

"This is not a minority district, you know," she says.

"I doubt if I have more than fifteen or twenty percent Hispanic, maybe one percent black. It's a definitely blue-collar district. I've got a lot of families that live in trailer parks, and truck farmers with small plots. We've got a variety of middle class here. Italian families that have been here for generations—they grow lettuce and corn and peppers. Mostly it's really working people, the working poor and middle-class workers."

From what we had read about Baca-Barragan's background in Chicano affairs and leadership, we had figured her constituency would be poor and Hispanic. "It's weird how people get impressions," she says. Baca-Barragan herself doesn't hold with any labels; she won't describe herself as liberal or conservative.

"I'm still very radical when it comes to things like Hispanic issues, Chicano issues, or female issues— civil rights issues—but I just don't publicize them. I publicize my tax positions, my positions on school finances and property taxes. My overall image is probably one of being a moderate, but that's only because I talk to the people I don't agree with. You know, from the time I graduated from college until the time I was elected, I cannot remember ever having a social drink with Republicans unless they were Chicanos. But now it's different. I'll sit down with them at Nick's and have a drink with them. I listen to both sides. That doesn't mean, after all, that I'll vote their way. I have my own free will. I just happen to hate cliques. I've got a problem with it because of what I went through, being assimilated and all that."

Baca-Barragan's family has lived in Colorado for four generations, and each generation has experienced discrimination. She grew up in Greeley, a small farming community northeast of Denver. Her father was a farm worker who owned no land, but they were not as poor as the migrants who came in every summer to work the fields. She says one of her earliest memories is how bigoted Anglos in Greeley were toward Chicanos. At the Catholic church she attended, Anglos sat in the middle pews while Chicanos had to sit on the sides. When she was three years old and in church one day, she wanted to get a closer look at some young Anglo girls receiving Holy Communion. She asked her mother to move up to the front center aisles. An usher came and made them move back. As Baca-Barragan tells you this, you see that the event burned an indelible imprint on her consciousness. "That was my first recollection of prejudice," she says.

Thinking that perhaps that experience had moved her toward political action for her people, we asked what her first real political act had been. "I've always been involved with politics," she said, "even as a child. The first thing I remember in politics was staying up all night with my father, listening to the 1948 returns. I was fascinated because everyone thought Dewey would win, and Daddy was for Truman; so of course I was for

Truman. I carried signs at school, and nobody else was
for Truman. But we won. And I remember that very
distinctly. I was about seven years old, and I was
fascinated by it, always have been. In 1956, I actually
did a little bit of work for Adlai Stevenson against
Eisenhower. I was in the ninth grade, and we formed a
Young Democrats club. We didn't do much, but it
was down on paper. And we got our names in the
newspaper. It was basically a Republican county. We
were always a minority there.

"It seems like I'm always a minority. In ninth grade,
I thought I wanted to be a lawyer, and I did a report on
it. And the one thing I got from the report was that a
woman did not become a lawyer. So instead of going
into history or civics, when I went to college (Colorado
State University), I started taking physics and chemistry. I decided to be the first woman on the moon. My
first major was in physics, but then, as a sophomore, I
got back involved in politics. But I don't think I ever
really thought I'd run for office. It was so far removed."

Like many young people her age, Baca-Barragan
went into politics because John F. Kennedy was
running for President. His call to youth to participate
in the electoral process brought out thousands of
volunteers in colleges throughout the country. Baca-
Barragan became the state college coordinator for the
Colorado *Viva Kennedy!* campaign, representing Hispanic supporters.

Although she recalls that at the time the idea of being a politician seemed "far removed," it's obvious that she enjoyed being in the center of things. Her love of politics wasn't satisfied by just working in another person's campaign.

"In college I ran for student-body offices. But I was always the secretary," she says, laughing. "I was the secretary of the freshman class, but you know, that was a big deal for me because I was a Chicano, and on an agricultural campus that blew everyone's mind to begin with. And then to be a woman—women just didn't run. I did become president of my college Young Democrats club. But that was just because the president was flunking out. And I had done a good job as vice president, putting on a mock nominating convention during the Kennedy campaign. It was very successful. My professors were so impressed by it that I got an internship with the Kennedy campaign, which is what really turned me on. I fell in love with that man. I was just totally, emotionally in love with him."

When she graduated from college in 1963, Baca-Barragan was listed in *Who's Who in American Colleges and Universities*. She took a job in Washington, D.C., working for a large union newspaper. Soon she got involved in Democratic politics there.

"I lost a whole bunch of stuff when I was in D.C. Everything I ran for, I lost. I ran for office in Young Democrats, and it was at the time that the black movement was coming in. They took over the Young Democrats club—SNCC [Student Nonviolent Coordinating Committee] did. I was offered a position on their slate, but I felt very loyal to the people I was involved with, so I took the other people, and we lost.

"Then I was a candidate for national committeewoman, and a black had never had it before. They ran a black woman against me, a young attorney. Wow, was she neat! It was the first time in my life that I ever felt like I was part of the majority, and I couldn't deal with it. It just wasn't right. I had always been the underdog."

In 1968, when Robert Kennedy ran for President in the primaries, Baca-Barragan was again drawn into full-time campaigning, but now with a higher position. She joined Kennedy's national campaign staff as assistant director of his *Viva Kennedy!* movement. She was in Los Angeles, working on the California primary for Kennedy, when he was shot.

"It was the lowest point in my life," she recalled. "I was with Cesar Chavez. We went through the kitchen door the assassin must have entered. We were on our way to the next floor. By the time we got there, it was all over. We couldn't believe it."

Robert Kennedy's death left a huge void in her life. She had identified the needs of her people with his candidacy. He was the first national politician who cared about Chicano problems—and he cared deeply.

The Chicano people returned the feeling. Thousands came to help him win the California primary. They knew that if he won, they would not be forgotten. Baca-Barragan must have known, too, that there would be a place for her in an RFK administration, or perhaps Kennedy support for her in whatever she might decide to do in the future.

As she talks, though, it is clear that she also truly loved the man and what he stood for. Then, suddenly, it was all over. Like many others who had worked closely with Bobby Kennedy, she temporarily lost her stomach for politics. Baca-Barragan traveled to South America, doing nothing in particular, trying, as she says, "to put the pieces of my life back together."

She seems to have gone through a process shared with other full-time workers in either the Kennedy or McCarthy campaigns that year. Realizing that there was no one else she wanted to work for, her thoughts led to "I might as well stand up myself for the thing I believe in." She decided to return to Colorado. By 1972 she was looking around for a Democratic district that offered the possibility of running for office someday. She figured it would take her about four years to become known in the community and then consolidate support for running. Thornton was close to where her parents lived, and she had other family nearby.

"My folks were probably one of the first Hispanic

families to move to the Thornton area, but then, a few years later, my aunt and uncle moved there too. Then I've got some cousins who came into the precinct. Now I must have about ten sets of cousins in my district, but they weren't there when I first came in."

She had thought she would run for the City Council first, but in 1974, two years ahead of her timetable, the Democratic nominee for state representative suddenly dropped out of the race. The seat was up for grabs, and it was understood that whoever was the Democratic candidate would most likely win the office. Polly Baca-Barragan and three others were interested in running.

The nominee was to be chosen by local Democratic committee people. At the time, eleven committee spots were vacant. The county chairman called all the candidates together and said that in order to be fair, he was not going to fill the vacancies. Each candidate could go out and try to fill the slots with his or her own supporters.

"I decided to fill all those eleven vacancies myself," Baca-Barragan says, "and the others just didn't bother. I got all my relatives to call people to try to find friends and neighbors, what have you, to find people that would take on a spot. I filled every single one of those vacancies, with the exception of one. I filled ten of them. But I made one mistake, and it caused some backlash. I didn't take into consideration the ethnic backgrounds of the people I was filling them with. Now, this not being a minority district, it looked a little bit odd when all of a sudden you had six people that were Chicanos, two Indians, an Asian-American, and a white woman. It was the only precinct in town like that.

"I had a very strong inner feeling that if I could get to every precinct committee person, I could talk them into supporting me. I just had the feeling that if I really worked hard, on a one-to-one basis, I could get their votes. I had this one committeeman, he lived in a mobile home, and I knew this and had really done my homework on mobile-home taxation. I walked into his home, and the first thing he said was, 'Are you one of those women libbers? I notice you don't wear a wedding band.' Well, I had stopped wearing a wedding band a long time ago because I was always losing it, so I had to defend my position in terms of it was just being practical. Then he went on to ask was I a militant. I kept trying to get back to the issue, mobile-home taxation, but he obviously thought that a woman's place was in the home.

"Later, at a debate in front of all the precinct committee people, one of my supporters went up to him and said, 'Now, Bill, what's your big issue? What have you been the most angry about?' He said, 'The mobile-home taxation,' muttering under his breath. She said, 'O.K., will you make an agreement with me?

Will you agree that whoever knows the most about mobile-home taxation and understands the issue, that you will commit yourself to that person?' He said, 'Yes, O.K. Sure,' feeling, I think, very confident that I would certainly not be the person.

"But when the issue came up in the debate, the other two just hadn't done their homework. But I had read the whole report on it, so I really came out strong on that. And Bill was literally embarrassed into voting for me. And it turned out he was my winning vote."

Baca-Barragan won the general election handily and took office in 1975.

As she recalls this first campaign on her own behalf, she speaks fast and excitedly, remembering every face and vote. Listening to her, we can see why she has been called a "powerhouse." You can hear the determination that made her go out and talk to each committee person and convince them to vote for her. She found out what each one of them was interested in and briefed herself on those subjects. This is what she has done as a legislator, too. Her bills cover a wide range of interests, from consumer protection to tax-code revision, from bilingual education programs to migrant workers to mobile-home owners. Part of her powerhouse quality comes from almost a compulsion to show her competence and knowledge on even the most technical and hard-to-understand issues. It seems linked somehow to the feeling that made her take physics and chemistry as college majors. Now, in describing her legislative interest, she talks to us with great enthusiasm about the most minute aspects of property assessment and tax-code provisions. At such moments, she seems a long way from our original conception of her (admittedly a cliché) as a radical Chicano woman activist.

We've been in her home for hours already, and Baca-Barragan shows no sign of wanting to stop, get rid of us, go back to whatever she might do on such an evening at home.

A little girl comes running downstairs, calling, "Mommy, mommy, they've picked the finalists." It's clear that before we arrived they had been watching the Miss Universe contest together. She introduces us to her daughter, and we all chat for a minute about the various candidates and her favorites. We start to feel like a part of this household, as if we are old friends who have worked with Baca-Barragan on other campaigns.

Baca-Barragan will not be pigeonholed. She's been a supporter of the Equal Rights Amendment and abortion rights—she's been strong on all aspects of civil rights; but she refuses to stand still long enough to become a symbol for any one issue, even among her own people.

"The Chicanos know where I'm at on Chicano issues," she says. "Like a bill I introduced to provide an emergency fund for farm laborers. It lost in the Senate. I lost that when I was two weeks from having a baby. People still remember that. I scared the senators because they were so worried about me—I was so upset about it. It was my Migratory Labor Bill. The act would have taken three hundred thousand dollars and set it aside so when a farm laborer had an accident, say, in one county, on his way to another county to work, he could take money out of the fund and use it for him and his family—to do whatever you had to do to help him and his car get to the county where his contract was to work. Quite frankly, I was hoping— and I did get some of the more conservative members to support it, on the basis that it was helping people to stay off the welfare rolls. But it was really a very radical piece of legislation, in the sense that it would have taken state money to help out a certain class of people—poor Chicanos, blacks, and Anglos—who were not even citizens of the state, maybe even not citizens of this country.

"This bill was not something my district would normally have supported. There are certain things that I know the people of this district would really like to see me do, and it's those things that I go out of my way to get publicity on. There are other things—if they find out about them, O.K., but they're not the kinds of things that are going to bring in votes, so I just don't publicize them. Anybody can check your voting record if they want to; and if the press wants to pick it up, fine. But they normally don't.

"I don't think it's easy to say what's liberal and conservative anymore. I'm very strong on feminist issues. I supported a bill that's very near and dear to my heart that would give unemployment compensation to women if they were dismissed from their jobs for pregnancy. Some Republican business people thought that was a radical thing. But overall, my image is one of being a moderate.

"When I was running for leadership in the House, there were two people running against me for Caucus chair—an Anglo male and a black woman. The black woman is viewed as being very militant. That's just her style. I bet anything that my voting record is more liberal than hers. And I won."

Winning is very important to Polly Baca-Barragan. She recalls her few past losses in great detail, and you sense that she's learned lessons from each of them. "In my entire years of running," she says, "I've only lost one precinct. That was my smallest precinct, in the last election, in 1976. I had two hundred people in that precinct. I was running against a real John Bircher. He was anti-ERA, anti-abortion, anti-women, anti-gun-control, anti-everything. He was just straight out a real nut. And I thought, 'This is just such a fool. Why waste putting on a real campaign?' So I ran a campaign, but not to the extent that I had before.

I had a problem with that one precinct, too. Every time I'd send campaign workers in there, they'd get bitten by dogs; all these people there had huge dogs. So I figured rather than take that chance, I decided not to walk it myself. And you know, I lost that precinct. Four years ago in '74, I didn't lose a single precinct. But I did this time. That's the only precinct I ever lost."

As we are interviewing her, Baca-Barragan is in the middle of a campaign for State Senate, which she will win, as there's no opponent. But she's still running hard, perhaps for something else her mind has seized upon already, further along on the political road.

"You don't really gain anything by losing, and I really don't like to lose. It really hurts. I've watched Jerry Brown and how he got to be governor. He started off with some sort of finky position, and then he built up to secretary of state of California, and then he went on to become governor. But he started out small. I've got lots of time. You know, when I was a child I never thought I'd meet a politician, let alone be one."

Elizabeth Levy has written many books for young people and adults, including, the widely-acclaimed *Struggle and Lose, Struggle and Win: The United Mineworkers Story.* A graduate of Pembroke College and Columbia University, she lives in New York City.

Mara Miller is a writer and researcher who has created program materials for numerous educational television series, including the award-winning "Our-story." A graduate of Sarah Lawrence College, Ms. Miller lives in New York City.